SPIRITUAL AND HOLISTIC WELLNESS

SPIRITUAL AND HOLISTIC WELLNESS

RAFEAL MECHLORE

ROSE PUBLISHING

Contents

INDEX	1
INTRODUCTION	3
Chapter 1	5
Chapter 2	19
Chapter 3	34
Chapter 4	49
Chapter 5	62
Chapter 6	73
Chapter 7	84
Chapter 8	94

INDEX

Chapter 1: Introduction to Holistic Wellness
1.1 Defining Holistic Wellness
1.2 Why Holistic Wellness Matters
1.3 The Journey Towards Balance

Chapter 2: Nurturing Your Mind
2.1 The Mind-Body Connection
2.2 Practices for Mental Clarity
2.3 Cultivating Mindfulness and Presence

Chapter 3: Fueling Your Body
3.1 Holistic Nutrition
3.2 The Role of Exercise
3.3 Rest and Sleep for Vitality

Chapter 4: Awakening Your Spirit
4.1 Spirituality and Holistic Health
4.2 Practices for Spiritual Growth
4.3 Finding Purpose and Connection

Chapter 5: Emotional Wellbeing
5.1 Understanding Emotions
5.2 Managing Stress and Anxiety
5.3 Cultivating Positive Emotions

Chapter 6: Holistic Healing Therapies
6.1 Complementary and Alternative Medicine
6.2 Energy Healing Modalities
6.3 Integrating Holistic Therapies

Chapter 7: Holistic Living
7.1 Creating a Holistic Home Environment
7.2 Sustainable Living Practices
7.3 Nurturing Relationships and Social Wellness

Chapter 8: The Holistic Journey Ahead
8.1 Overcoming Challenges
8.2 Sustaining Holistic Wellness
8.3 Holistic Wellness as a Lifelong Path

INTRODUCTION

In the fast-paced world we inhabit, where the demands of daily life can often feel overwhelming, it has become increasingly vital to seek balance and harmony within ourselves. In this pursuit of a fulfilling and meaningful existence, the concept of spiritual and holistic wellness has emerged as a beacon of hope. As we delve into the depths of this multifaceted approach to well-being, we embark on a transformative journey that transcends the physical realm, nurturing not only our bodies but also our minds and spirits. This journey invites us to explore the profound interconnectedness of our being and discover the infinite potential for growth and healing that resides within us.

At its core, spiritual and holistic wellness is a philosophy that acknowledges the intricate relationship between the physical, emotional, mental, and spiritual aspects of our lives. It advocates for the cultivation of a deep sense of awareness and balance in these dimensions, fostering a state of wholeness that goes beyond mere absence of illness or stress. Instead, it encourages us to flourish, to thrive, and to lead lives that are rich in purpose and fulfillment.

The spiritual dimension of this wellness paradigm transcends religious affiliations and dogmas. It is about connecting with the essence of our inner selves, seeking answers to profound questions about existence, meaning, and purpose. It encourages us to explore the depths of our consciousness, often through practices like meditation, mindfulness, or prayer, and to cultivate a sense of inner peace and tranquility. By nurturing our spirituality, we open ourselves to a wellspring of wisdom and inner strength that can guide us through life's challenges and uncertainties.

Holistic wellness complements the spiritual dimension by emphasizing the interplay between the physical, emotional, and mental aspects of our well-being. It recognizes that our bodies are not isolated vessels but integral parts of a complex system. Thus, it encourages us to adopt a comprehensive approach to health that considers not only our physical fitness but also our emotional resilience and mental clarity. Exercise, nutrition, and rest are essential components, but so are self-care practices, emotional intelligence, and stress management.

One of the remarkable aspects of spiritual and holistic wellness is its inclusivity.

It accommodates a diverse range of practices and beliefs, making it accessible to people of all backgrounds and walks of life. Whether you find solace in ancient wisdom traditions, seek guidance from modern psychology, or draw inspiration from a combination of sources, there is a place for you on this transformative journey. It encourages us to be open-minded, to explore, and to adapt, inviting us to weave our own unique tapestry of wellness.

Moreover, the benefits of spiritual and holistic wellness extend far beyond individual well-being. As we embark on this journey of self-discovery and self-improvement, we often find that our relationships with others also flourish. Our newfound sense of inner peace and emotional resilience equips us to navigate conflicts with grace and compassion. We become better listeners, more empathetic partners, and sources of support for those around us. In turn, our communities and societies benefit from this ripple effect of positivity and healing.

In this exploration of spiritual and holistic wellness, we will delve into the key principles and practices that constitute this transformative journey. We will discuss the importance of self-awareness, the role of mindfulness and meditation, the significance of nutrition and exercise, and the profound impact of emotional and mental well-being. Through these discussions, we aim to provide a comprehensive guide that empowers individuals to embark on their own path to wholeness and vitality.

As we embark on this journey together, may we discover the richness and depth that spiritual and holistic wellness can bring to our lives. May we find solace in the interconnectedness of our being, and may we learn to nurture and cherish the most precious gift we possess: ourselves. Ultimately, by embracing spiritual and holistic wellness, we take a step closer to living a life that is not only healthy but also deeply fulfilling and meaningful.

Chapter 1

Introduction to Holistic Wellness

During a time set apart by quick mechanical progressions, steady cultural requests, and a consistently speeding up speed of life, the quest for comprehensive wellbeing has arisen as a basic for those trying to accomplish equilibrium, satisfaction, and a more profound association with themselves and their general surroundings. All encompassing health is an exhaustive way to deal with wellbeing and prosperity that recognizes the multifaceted transaction between the physical, mental, close to home, and profound parts of our lives. It perceives that genuine prosperity reaches out past simple shortfall of disease or actual wellness and embraces a significant feeling of completeness and imperativeness that envelops each feature of our reality.

At its center, all encompassing health welcomes us to reexamine our lives, to stop and ponder our decisions, and to perceive the significant effect of these decisions on our general wellbeing and bliss. It is an update that our prosperity not set in stone by outer factors like hereditary qualities or climate yet is significantly impacted by the cognizant choices we make in regards to our ways of life, convictions, and mentalities.

The Underlying foundations of All encompassing Wellbeing

The idea of all encompassing wellbeing is well established in antiquated astuteness and customary recuperating rehearses that date back hundreds of years. All through mankind's set of experiences, societies all over the planet have perceived the interconnectedness of the psyche, body, and soul, and have created comprehensive frameworks of medication and prosperity to encourage wellbeing and concordance.

One of the earliest articulations of all encompassing wellbeing can be tracked down in the acts of Ayurveda, the antiquated Indian arrangement of medication. Ayurveda, and that signifies "information on life," sees wellbeing as a condition of harmony between the body, brain, and soul. It accentuates the significance of customized, regular treatments, including dietary decisions, home grown cures, reflection, and yoga, to accomplish and keep up with prosperity.

Essentially, Customary Chinese Medication (TCM) is established on the guideline of harmony between the contradicting powers of yin and yang inside the body, as well as the progression of indispensable energy, or Qi. TCM incorporates needle therapy,

natural medication, and practices like Judo and Qigong, all intended to blend the body's energies and advance comprehensive health.

Native mending customs from different societies additionally underscore the significance of profound and close to home prosperity in actual wellbeing. Local American medication, for example, perceives the holiness of the normal world and the significant association among people and their current circumstance.

The Cutting edge Resurgence of All encompassing Wellbeing

While comprehensive wellbeing has profound verifiable roots, its resurgence in the cutting edge time can be credited to a blend of variables. The 20th century saw wonderful progressions in clinical science, which prompted a more noteworthy comprehension of illnesses and their medicines. In any case, this progress likewise uncovered the restrictions of a reductionist way to deal with wellbeing, which frequently centered around treating explicit side effects as opposed to tending to the underlying drivers of disease.

As people looked for options in contrast to ordinary medication, they rediscovered the all encompassing methodologies of antiquated customs. The nonconformity developments of the 1960s and 1970s assumed a critical part in promoting comprehensive health rehearses in the West. These developments underscored self-improvement, otherworldliness, and an all encompassing perspective on wellbeing that resounded with an age looking for importance past realism.

The developing interest in all encompassing health corresponded with a change in standard medication towards integrative and reciprocal treatments. Numerous medical services experts started to perceive the benefit of joining ordinary medication with all encompassing ways to deal with accomplish better understanding results. This affirmation legitimized all encompassing health and prepared for its more extensive acknowledgment.

The Mainstays of All encompassing Health

At the core of all encompassing health lie a few essential rules that guide people on their way to prosperity. These standards act as a system for understanding the comprehensive way to deal with wellbeing and proposition experiences into how it tends to be applied in commonsense terms.

1. **Completeness and Mix**

    All encompassing wellbeing sees people as complete and incorporated creatures. It underscores that our physical, mental, close to home, and otherworldly aspects are interconnected, and our general prosperity relies upon the amicable working of this

    large number of angles. It isn't sufficient to zero in exclusively on one aspect

while ignoring others; genuine prosperity emerges from sustaining and coordinating all aspects.
2. **Mind-Body Association**
   An essential precept of all encompassing wellbeing is the acknowledgment of the significant association between the psyche and the body. It recognizes that our contemplations, feelings, and convictions impact our actual wellbeing, and alternately, our actual wellbeing influences our psychological and close to home states. This brain body association shapes the reason for different all encompassing practices pointed toward advancing congruity between these aspects.
3. **Mindfulness and Self-Obligation**
   All encompassing health puts serious areas of strength for an on mindfulness and self-obligation. It welcomes people to become aware of their decisions, ways of behaving, and thought designs. Through mindfulness, we gain bits of knowledge into what our choices mean for our prosperity. Assuming self-liability implies effectively settling on decisions that line up with our qualities and goals, perceiving that our prosperity is eventually our own liability.
4. **All encompassing Recuperating Modalities**
   All encompassing health embraces a wide cluster of recuperating modalities and practices. These reach from antiquated customs like needle therapy, home grown medication, and contemplation to contemporary methodologies, for example, chiropractic care, wholesome treatment, and energy mending. Every methodology offers one of a kind devices and viewpoints for advancing prosperity and tending to explicit wellbeing concerns.
5. **Otherworldliness and Internal Association**

Otherworldliness is a focal part of all encompassing health, yet it reaches out past strict convictions. It includes a feeling of inward association, reason, and greatness. Otherworldliness welcomes people to investigate inquiries of importance and importance, encouraging a more profound comprehension of their spot in the universe and their interconnectedness with all of presence.

The Significance of All encompassing Wellbeing in Present day Life

In the high speed, mechanically determined, and frequently unpleasant universe of the 21st 100 years, the pertinence of all encompassing wellbeing turns out to be

progressively apparent. It tends to a large number of the difficulties and worries that people face in their regular routines.

1. **Stress and Emotional wellness**
   Stress has turned into an unavoidable and concerning part of present day life. The requests of work, prevalent difficulties, and the steady flood of data can prompt ongoing pressure, uneasiness, and burnout. All encompassing

health offers procedures to oversee pressure, develop profound flexibility, and accomplish mental clearness.

2. **Persistent Infection and Actual Wellbeing**
Ongoing illnesses like coronary illness, diabetes, and stoutness have arrived at plague extents. A considerable lot of these circumstances are established in way of life factors, including terrible eating routine, absence of actual work, and high-feelings of anxiety. All encompassing wellbeing stresses preventive measures, empowering nutritious eating, ordinary activity, and psyche body practices to help actual wellbeing.

3. **Advanced Over-burden and Disengagement**
The computerized age has brought various comforts, yet it has likewise added to a feeling of disengagement from ourselves as well as other people. Exorbitant screen time, virtual entertainment, and steady network can prompt sensations of confinement and shallow connections. Comprehensive health urges people to turn off, reconnect with their internal identities, and cultivate significant associations with others.

4. **The Quest for Importance**

In a materialistic culture that frequently focuses on outer achievement, numerous people wind up longing for more profound significance and reason throughout everyday life. All encompassing health gives a system to investigating otherworldliness and inward association, assisting people with finding a feeling of direction past the quest for riches and status.

The Comprehensive Wellbeing Excursion

As we leave on the excursion of investigating all encompassing health, it's vital to perceive that it's anything but an objective however a continuous way of self-disclosure and development. An excursion welcomes people to dig into the profundities of their being, interface with the insight of their bodies, sustain their profound prosperity, and stir their spirits. An excursion engages people to assume responsibility for their wellbeing

and satisfaction, to live with expectation and reason, and to find congruity in a world frequently portrayed by confusion and interruption.

All through the parts of this investigation, we will dig further into the different elements of comprehensive health, offering bits of knowledge, reasonable activities, and direction to help self-awareness and prosperity. We will investigate the brain body association, dive into comprehensive sustenance, find the force of otherworldly practices, and reveal the insider facts of profound flexibility. We will likewise investigate the rich embroidery of comprehensive recuperating modalities and systems for making an all encompassing way of life that lines up with individual qualities and desires.

As we embrace this excursion, recollect that comprehensive health is definitely not a one-size-fits-all methodology. It welcomes people to embrace their remarkable ways, perceiving that what reverberates most profoundly with one individual might contrast from another. It is an excursion of self-revelation and strengthening, and each step taken carries us more like a more adjusted, energetic, and satisfying life.

Thus, let us leave on this excursion together, with open hearts and receptive outlooks, as we investigate the immense and groundbreaking scene of all encompassing health and find its significant effect on our lives.

1.1 Defining Holistic Wellness

In a world portrayed by the intricacies of current life, where stress, disengagement, and the steady quest for outer achievement frequently eclipse our inward prosperity, the idea of comprehensive health has arisen as an encouraging sign and a way towards a more adjusted, satisfied, and significant presence. All encompassing health addresses a thorough way to deal with wellbeing and prosperity that rises above the limits of conventional medication and embraces a more extensive point of view — one that recognizes the many-sided interchange between the physical, mental, close to home, and profound parts of our lives.

At its center, all encompassing wellbeing welcomes us to see ourselves as multilayered creatures, perceiving that our prosperity not entirely set in stone by our actual wellbeing however is profoundly entwined with the condition of our psyches, feelings, and our feeling of direction and association. In this investigation, we will dig into the key standards and parts that characterize all encompassing health and comprehend the reason why it has turned into a fundamental way of thinking in the present high speed world.

The Substance of All encompassing Wellbeing

Comprehensive wellbeing is established in the comprehension that people are entire creatures, more prominent than the amount of their parts. It recognizes that every individual is an interesting blend of physical, mental, profound, and otherworldly features, and that these features are personally interconnected. Comprehensive health

states that prosperity can't be accomplished by disconnecting and treating one aspect while overlooking the others. All things being equal, it requires an amicable reconciliation of all parts of oneself.

Actual Health

Actual health is the primary part of comprehensive prosperity. It incorporates the condition of one's actual wellbeing and imperativeness. It includes sustaining the body through practices like customary activity, appropriate sustenance, sufficient rest, and preventive medical services. Actual wellbeing isn't exclusively about the shortfall of sickness yet the presence of strong wellbeing and energy that permits people to connect completely in their lives.

Mental Wellbeing

Mental wellbeing relates to the soundness of the brain. It includes developing mental clearness, close to home flexibility, and mental readiness. Mental health empowers the improvement of positive idea designs, stress the board abilities, and the capacity to adjust and flourish even with life's difficulties. It perceives the indivisible association between the brain and the body, where psychological well-being impacts actual wellbeing as well as the other way around.

Profound Health

Close to home health fixates on the comprehension and the executives of one's feelings. It includes the ability to distinguish and communicate sentiments in a solid and useful way. Close to home wellbeing supports mindfulness, the capacity to appreciate people on a deeper level, and the capacity to explore the full range of feelings, from delight and love to misery and outrage. It recognizes that close to home prosperity significantly influences one's general personal satisfaction.

Otherworldly Wellbeing

Otherworldly wellbeing envelops the domain of the internal identity, one's feeling of direction, and the mission for importance throughout everyday life. It doesn't be guaranteed to relate to strict convictions yet rather to a more profound association with the universe, a feeling of greatness, and an investigation of the secrets of presence.

Otherworldly wellbeing welcomes people to look for inward harmony, find their life's motivation, and adjust their activities to their guiding principle.

The Standards of Comprehensive Wellbeing

To really get a handle on the pith of all encompassing health, it is fundamental to comprehend the rules that support this way of thinking. These standards act as directing lights, enlightening the way towards a reasonable and agreeable life.

Completeness and Coordination

The guideline of completeness and mix shapes the bedrock of comprehensive wellbeing. It accentuates that people are finished creatures, and genuine prosperity is accomplished through the mix and congruity of all components of oneself. Completeness recognizes that the psyche, body, feelings, and soul are interconnected and associated.

Mind-Body Association

Key to all encompassing health is the acknowledgment of the significant association between the brain and the body. This rule attests that our psychological and close to home states fundamentally influence our actual wellbeing. It highlights the significance of practices that advance an agreeable connection between the psyche and the body, like reflection, care, and stress decrease procedures.

Mindfulness and Self-Obligation

Comprehensive wellbeing puts areas of strength for an on mindfulness and self-obligation. It welcomes people to become aware of their decisions, ways of behaving, and thought designs. Through mindfulness, people gain experiences into how their choices impact their prosperity. Self-obligation implies playing a functioning job in pursuing decisions that line up with one's qualities and desires.

All encompassing Mending Modalities

All encompassing wellbeing embraces a different exhibit of recuperating modalities and practices. These envelop antiquated customs like needle therapy, home grown medication, and reflection, as well as contemporary methodologies, for example, chiropractic care, wholesome treatment, and energy recuperating. These modalities offer novel instruments and points of view for advancing prosperity and tending to explicit wellbeing concerns.

Otherworldliness and Inward Association

Otherworldliness assumes a focal part in comprehensive wellbeing. Nonetheless, otherworldliness inside this setting isn't restricted to strict convictions yet envelops a feeling of inward association and reason. It welcomes people to investigate inquiries of importance, amazing quality, and their interconnectedness with the universe.

The Cutting edge Importance of All encompassing Wellbeing

In the present high speed and carefully determined world, the importance of all encompassing wellbeing has never been more articulated. It tends to the squeezing difficulties and worries that people face in their regular routines and offers a structure for exploring the intricacies of the 21st 100 years.

Stress and Emotional well-being

Ongoing pressure, uneasiness, and emotional wellness issues have become unavoidable in present day culture. The requests of work, cultural tensions, and the consistent convergence of data can overpower people. Comprehensive wellbeing gives techniques to overseeing pressure, upgrading flexibility, and cultivating mental clearness and profound equilibrium.

Persistent Illness and Actual Wellbeing

Persistent illnesses, like coronary illness, diabetes, and stoutness, have arrived at scourge extents. A considerable lot of these circumstances are established in way of life factors, including less than stellar eating routine, stationary way of behaving, and high-feelings of anxiety. Comprehensive wellbeing underlines preventive measures, advancing nutritious eating, ordinary active work, and brain body practices to help in general actual wellbeing.

Innovation and Separation

While innovation has brought various comforts, it has likewise added to a feeling of separation from ourselves as well as other people. Inordinate screen time, web-based entertainment, and advanced interruptions can prompt sensations of seclusion and shallow connections. Comprehensive health urges people to turn off, reconnect with their internal identities, and cultivate significant associations with others.

The Quest for Importance

In a materialistic culture that frequently focuses on outer achievement, numerous people end up longing for more profound significance and reason throughout everyday life. Comprehensive wellbeing gives a structure to investigating otherworldliness and internal association, assisting people with finding a feeling of direction past the quest for riches and status.

The Comprehensive Health Excursion

The excursion of all encompassing wellbeing isn't an objective yet a continuous investigation of self-revelation and self-awareness. It welcomes people to dive into the

profundities of their being, associate with the insight of their bodies, sustain their profound prosperity, and stir their spirits. It enables people to assume responsibility for their wellbeing and satisfaction, to live with goal and reason, and to find concordance in a world frequently portrayed by mayhem and interruption.

As we set out on this excursion, it is fundamental to perceive that all encompassing health is a profoundly private way. It welcomes people to embrace their interesting excursions and inclinations, perceiving that what reverberates most profoundly with one individual might contrast from another. It is an excursion of self-revelation and strengthening, and each step taken carries us more like a more adjusted, dynamic, and satisfying life.

In the parts that follow, we will dive further into the different components of all encompassing health, offering experiences, useful activities, and direction to help self-improvement and prosperity. We will investigate the psyche body association, dig into comprehensive sustenance, find the force of otherworldly practices, and uncover the insider facts of close to home strength. We will likewise investigate the rich embroidery of comprehensive mending modalities and procedures for making an all encompassing way of life that lines up with individual qualities and goals.

As we embrace this excursion, let us do as such with open hearts and receptive outlooks, as we investigate the immense and groundbreaking scene of comprehensive health and find its significant effect on our lives.

1.2 Why Holistic Wellness Matters

In the rushing about of current life, where the constant quest for progress, material riches, and outer accomplishments frequently becomes the dominant focal point, the idea of all encompassing wellbeing arises as a basic and extraordinary offset. Comprehensive wellbeing rises above the limited bounds of actual wellbeing and customary medication, offering a thorough and incorporated way to deal with prosperity that includes the sum of the human experience — body, psyche, feelings, and soul. Understanding the reason why all encompassing wellbeing matters is fundamental in this present reality where stress, disengagement, and the disintegration of our inward concordance have become progressively pervasive.

1. **An Extensive Way to deal with Wellbeing**

    All encompassing health perceives that people are not only actual bodies with mechanical capabilities but rather multi-faceted creatures. It recognizes that prosperity can't be accomplished by tending to one part of the self in separation. All things considered, it requires the amicable coordination of all elements of life: physical, mental,

    profound, and otherworldly. This far reaching way to deal with wellbeing guarantees that people experience essentialness and equilibrium in each aspect of their reality.

Customary medical services frequently centers around the therapy of explicit side effects or illnesses, ignoring the fundamental causes and the interconnected idea of wellbeing. Comprehensive wellbeing, then again, endeavors to distinguish and address the underlying drivers of lopsidedness, perceiving that side effects might be appearances of more profound issues in different components of life.

2. **Mind-Body Association**

   All encompassing wellbeing puts areas of strength for an on the complicated and indivisible association between the psyche and the body. It perceives that our psychological and close to home states essentially influence our actual wellbeing, as well as the other way around. This standard recognizes that pressure, nervousness, and pessimistic idea examples can prompt actual infirmities, while actual wellbeing practices can decidedly impact mental and profound prosperity.

   Understanding and sustaining the brain body association empowers people to settle on cognizant decisions that advance generally speaking prosperity. Rehearses like contemplation, care, and stress the board strategies are essential parts of all encompassing health, cultivating a reasonable connection between the psyche and the body.

3. **Preventive Wellbeing and Health**

   One of the center precepts of all encompassing wellbeing is the accentuation on preventive wellbeing measures. Instead of trusting that ailment will show and afterward looking for treatment, comprehensive wellbeing urges people to find proactive ways to keep up with their wellbeing and forestall infection. This proactive methodology incorporates embracing a decent eating routine, taking part in standard actual work, overseeing pressure, and consolidating rehearses that help mental and close to home strength.

   By zeroing in on counteraction, people can lessen the gamble of constant sicknesses, improve their essentialness, and partake in a better of life. Preventive wellbeing measures line up with the way of thinking of all encompassing health, which values prosperity as a continuous and proactive excursion.

4. **Profound Strength and Mental Lucidity**

   In an undeniably quick moving and distressing world, close to home flexibility and mental lucidity are priceless resources. All encompassing health furnishes people with instruments and practices to explore the intricacies of existence with more prominent ability to understand anyone on a profound level and smartness. By encouraging
   mindfulness and close to home prosperity, all encompassing wellbeing prepares people to answer difficulties with strength, versatility, and a feeling of inward harmony.

Close to home flexibility permits people to return from misfortune, adapt to pressure all the more really, and keep an uplifting perspective even despite troubles. This close to home courage adds to worked on emotional well-being and a more noteworthy feeling of by and large prosperity.

5. **Importance and Reason**

Comprehensive wellbeing perceives the significance of otherworldliness and inward association in cultivating a feeling of importance and reason throughout everyday life. In a world frequently described by realism and outside accomplishments, people might wind up longing for more profound importance and a feeling of having a place with an option that could be more significant than themselves.

Otherworldly wellbeing, as a part of comprehensive health, urges people to investigate inquiries of importance, greatness, and the interconnectedness of all life. It gives a system to interfacing with one's internal identity, figuring out one's life's motivation, and adjusting one's activities to guiding principle.

6. **Feasible Way of life Decisions**

Comprehensive wellbeing supports feasible way of life decisions that benefit people as well as the planet. It underscores the significance of embracing eco-accommodating practices, careful utilization, and a profound regard for the normal world. Reasonable living lines up with the more extensive idea of all encompassing health, perceiving that singular prosperity is unpredictably connected to the prosperity of the planet.

By taking on manageable practices, people add to the protection of the climate, lessen their environmental impression, and advance worldwide prosperity. This comprehensive methodology expands the advantages of wellbeing past the person to envelop the more extensive biological system.

7. **Connections and Association**

All encompassing health recognizes the meaning of sustaining connections and cultivating significant associations with others. Sound social associations and strong connections are fundamental parts of prosperity. All encompassing health urges people to focus on association, correspondence, and sympathy in their cooperations with others.

By developing sound connections, people make an emotionally supportive network that adds to their profound and mental health. Social associations offer a feeling of having a place, decrease sensations of segregation, and improve in general life fulfillment.

8. **Flexibility in an Impacting World**

The world is continually advancing, introducing new difficulties and vulnerabilities. All encompassing wellbeing furnishes people with the strength and flexibility expected to flourish in a steadily evolving climate. By encouraging physical, mental, and close to home prosperity, comprehensive wellbeing assists people with exploring life's high points and low points with effortlessness and balance.

In a quickly impacting world, the capacity to adjust and keep up with prosperity is a precious resource. Comprehensive health furnishes people with the apparatuses and practices to confront vulnerability with certainty and flexibility.

9. **Strengthening and Self-awareness**

   All encompassing health enables people to play a functioning job in their own prosperity. It underscores mindfulness, self-obligation, and the capacity to settle on informed decisions that line up with one's qualities and goals. This strengthening encourages self-improvement and self-realization, permitting people to arrive at their maximum capacity.

   By embracing all encompassing health, people become dynamic members in their own excursion towards prosperity. They gain the certainty to settle on decisions that help their actual wellbeing, mental lucidity, close to home flexibility, and profound development.

10. **All encompassing Wellbeing as a Long lasting Excursion**

Maybe perhaps of the most convincing motivation behind why comprehensive wellbeing matters is that it is a deep rooted venture. It's anything but an objective to be reached yet a constant investigation of self-revelation, development, and change. All encompassing health welcomes people to embrace the consistently developing nature of prosperity, perceiving that it is a dynamic and continuous interaction.

As people venture along the way of comprehensive wellbeing, they develop a more profound comprehension of themselves and their general surroundings. They uncover the interconnectedness of all parts of life and experience a significant feeling of concordance, equilibrium, and satisfaction.

1.3 The Journey Towards Balance

In a world set apart by steady movement, tenacious requests, and the perpetual quest for progress, the mission for balance has turned into a general goal. The excursion towards balance is a profoundly private and frequently extraordinary way, one that welcomes people to explore the intricacies of current life while sustaining their physical, mental, close to home, and otherworldly prosperity. This excursion isn't an objective yet

a continuous investigation, a dance between different features of life, and a mission to orchestrate the various elements of our reality.

The Quest for Harmony

The idea of equilibrium is characteristic for how we might interpret congruity and prosperity. It summons pictures of balance, soundness, and the interchange between contradicting powers. Similarly as a tightrope walker endeavors to keep up with balance while crossing a thin rope high over the ground, people look to find their harmony in the difficult exercise of life.

The Lopsidedness of Current Life

In the cutting edge world, the sizes of equilibrium frequently slant dubiously. The requests of work, the tensions of day to day obligations, and the consistent barrage of data from the computerized age can disturb the harmony of life. Therefore, people might end up trapped in a never-ending condition of unevenness, attempting to accommodate their different jobs and obligations.

The outcomes of this awkwardness are expansive. It can appear as ongoing pressure, burnout, crumbling actual wellbeing, stressed connections, and an unavoidable feeling of disappointment. Perceiving the requirement for balance, people set out on a groundbreaking excursion towards harmony.

The Components of Equilibrium

Balance envelops numerous components of life, every one of which assumes a fundamental part in encouraging prosperity. The excursion towards balance includes blending these aspects to make an all encompassing and satisfying life.

Actual Equilibrium

Actual equilibrium alludes to the harmony of the body. It includes keeping up with actual wellbeing, imperativeness, and energy. Rehearses that advance actual equilibrium incorporate normal activity, legitimate nourishment, satisfactory rest, and preventive

medical care. Actual equilibrium guarantees that people have the actual endurance and flexibility to connect completely in their lives.

Mental Equilibrium

Mental equilibrium relates to the condition of the psyche. It includes developing mental lucidity, close to home flexibility, and mental nimbleness. Rehearses that help mental equilibrium incorporate care, reflection, stress the executives, and positive idea designs.

Mental equilibrium empowers people to think plainly, settle on informed choices, and explore the intricacies of existence with composure.

Profound Equilibrium

Close to home equilibrium fixates on the dominance of one's feelings. It envelops the ability to distinguish, express, and direct sentiments in a solid and valuable way. Rehearses that cultivate profound equilibrium incorporate capacity to understand individuals on a deeper level, mindfulness, and procedures for overseeing pressure and close to home reactivity. Profound equilibrium engages people to explore their feelings with effortlessness and validness.

Otherworldly Equilibrium

Otherworldly equilibrium relates to the inward elements of life, incorporating one's feeling of direction, internal harmony, and association with an option that could be more prominent than oneself. It isn't restricted to strict convictions however reaches out to a more profound comprehension of one's spot in the universe. Rehearses that advance otherworldly equilibrium incorporate self-reflection, contemplation, demonstrations of administration, and investigation of existential inquiries. Otherworldly equilibrium brings a significant feeling of importance and greatness to life.

Way of life Equilibrium

Way of life balance includes individuals decisions in their day to day routines. It incorporates viewpoints, for example, balance between serious and fun activities, using time effectively, and maintainable living practices. Accomplishing way of life balance expects people to adjust their activities to their qualities, focus on taking care of oneself, and pursue cognizant decisions that help their general prosperity.

The Excursion Towards Equilibrium

The excursion towards balance is a dynamic and steadily developing interaction. It's anything but a one-size-fits-all way yet rather a profoundly private investigation directed by one's qualities, goals, and exceptional conditions. This excursion unfurls in stages, every one of which adds to a more profound comprehension of equilibrium and prosperity.

1. **Self-Reflection and Mindfulness**

   The excursion towards offset starts with self-reflection and mindfulness. People should carve out opportunity to survey their present status of prosperity, distinguish areas of irregularity, and figure out the basic causes. Mindfulness is the establishment
   whereupon the excursion is constructed, giving the bits of knowledge expected to make the primary strides towards balance.

2. **Laying out Boundaries and Values**

   When people gain lucidity about their present status of equilibrium, they can start to lay out boundaries and adjust their activities to their qualities. This stage includes going with cognizant decisions about what makes the biggest difference throughout everyday life and focusing on the quest for those needs. It might include reprioritizing balance between serious and fun activities, reevaluating individual objectives, and dispensing with exercises or responsibilities that never again work well for one's being.

3. **Executing Functional Procedures**

   Accomplishing balance requires the execution of reasonable systems and way of life changes. This stage includes taking on rehearses that help physical, mental, profound, and otherworldly prosperity. People might integrate workout schedules, dietary changes, care practices, or stress the board methods into their regular routines. These procedures are the structure blocks of equilibrium, assisting people with recapturing harmony.

4. **Exploring Difficulties and Changes**

   The excursion towards balance isn't without its difficulties. Life is loaded up with startling turns, difficulties, and requests that can disturb even the most deeply grounded schedules. During this stage, people figure out how to explore

these difficulties with versatility and adaptability. They adjust their systems, look for help when required, and stay focused on their general prosperity.
5. **Developing Care and Presence**
Care and presence are fundamental parts of equilibrium. They include living right now, completely encountering every part of life as it unfurls. Developing care and presence permits people to enjoy the excellence of life, diminish pressure, and pursue purposeful decisions that line up with their qualities.
6. **Encouraging Significance and Association**
The excursion towards balance arrives at its finish in the development of significance and association. This stage includes developing one's profound mindfulness, investigating inquiries of direction, and supporting associations with others and the world. It is a phase of greatness, where people track down satisfaction past the quest for outer achievement.
7. **Embracing Deep rooted Learning**

Balance is definitely not a static state yet a continuous course of development and learning. People on the excursion towards balance embrace long lasting learning, constantly looking for new bits of knowledge and practices that improve their prosperity. They stay open to change, transformation, and the advancement of how they might interpret balance.

The Groundbreaking Force of Equilibrium

The excursion towards balance is a groundbreaking interaction that reaches out past the person to include the prosperity of everyone around them and the more extensive world. Adjusted people are better prepared to help and inspire others, cultivating amicable connections and contributing emphatically to their networks.

Additionally, the quest for balance can possibly swell outward, affecting cultural standards and values. As additional people focus on equilibrium and prosperity, a social shift happens, underlining the significance of all encompassing wellbeing over persevering desire and realism. This shift can prompt a more adjusted and amicable society, where the quest for harmony is esteemed as a way towards a satisfying life.

Chapter 2

Nurturing Your Mind

In the present high speed and complex world, supporting your psyche is fundamental for keeping up with in general prosperity. Our brains are the control communities of our lives, impacting our considerations, feelings, ways of behaving, and, surprisingly, our actual wellbeing. Mental health includes profound strength, mental clearness, and the capacity to explore life's difficulties with elegance and reason.

In this exhaustive aide, we will investigate the significance of sustaining your psyche and give an abundance of methodologies and practices to advance mental health. From care and stress the board to self-empathy and long lasting learning, these procedures are intended to assist you with developing a better and more adjusted mind.

Grasping Mental Wellbeing

Before we dive into explicit systems, it's critical to comprehend what mental health is and why it makes a difference.

What Is Mental Wellbeing?

Mental health, frequently alluded to as emotional well-being or personal prosperity, is a condition of mental and close to home prosperity wherein an individual can successfully oversee pressure, keep up with satisfying connections, work gainfully, and pursue informed choices. It envelops a scope of variables, including:

Profound Flexibility: The capacity to return from affliction and adapt to life's difficulties.

The ability to appreciate people on a deeper level: The ability to comprehend and deal with one's own feelings and the feelings of others.

Mental Lucidity: The capacity to think plainly, decide, and take care of issues really.

Positive Connections: Building and keeping up with sound, strong, and satisfying associations with others.

Reason and Significance: Discovering a feeling of direction, satisfaction, and fulfillment throughout everyday life.

For what reason Does Mental Wellbeing Matter?

Worked on Personal satisfaction: Mental health upgrades life fulfillment, joy, and by and large prosperity.

Viable Adapting: It outfits people with the instruments to adapt to pressure, difficulty, and life's difficulties.

Positive Connections: Great psychological wellness cultivates better, more significant associations with others.

Upgraded Efficiency: It can prompt expanded efficiency, imagination, and better direction.

Actual Wellbeing: Mental wellbeing is firmly associated with actual wellbeing, influencing insusceptible capability, cardiovascular wellbeing, and life span.

Self-improvement: It upholds self-improvement, self-completion, and a more profound comprehension of oneself and the world.

Now that we comprehend the significance of mental health, we should investigate different methodologies and practices to sustain your psyche.

Techniques for Sustaining Your Psyche

1. **Care and Contemplation**

   Care

   Care is a psychological practice that includes giving purposeful consideration to the current second without judgment. It urges you to turn out to be completely mindful of your viewpoints, feelings, sensations, and environmental factors. Rehearsing care can:

   Decrease pressure and tension.

   Further develop concentration and fixation.

   Improve profound guideline.

   Increment mindfulness.

   Advance a feeling of quiet and inward harmony.

   Step by step instructions to Practice Care:

   Find a peaceful spot where you will not be upset.

   Sit or rests serenely.

   Shut your eyes (if agreeable) and take a couple of full breaths.

   Carry your regard for your breath. Notice the vibe of every breath without attempting to change it.

   On the off chance that your psyche meanders, delicately take your concentration back to your breath.

   Step by step grow your attention to different sensations in your body, sounds, and the climate.

   Practice for just 5-10 minutes every day and steadily increment the term.

   Reflection

Adoring Graciousness Reflection (Metta): Develops sensations of affection, empathy, and generosity towards oneself as well as other people.

Body Sweep Reflection: Includes efficiently zeroing in on various pieces of the body to deliver pressure and advance unwinding.

Supernatural Contemplation (TM): Uses a particular mantra to accomplish a covert government of unwinding and elevated mindfulness.

Directed Contemplation: Includes paying attention to a recorded reflection drove by an educator.

Instructions to Begin Thinking:

Track down a tranquil and agreeable space.

Pick a reflection strategy or style that impacts you.

Sit or rests in a casual position.

Shut your eyes and start your picked contemplation practice.

Show restraint toward yourself; it might require investment to encounter the full advantages of contemplation.

2. **Developing Appreciation**

Expanding sensations of bliss and happiness.

Decreasing side effects of discouragement.

Improving life fulfillment.

Advancing an uplifting perspective on life.

The most effective method to Develop Appreciation:

Begin an Appreciation Diary: Consistently record three things you're thankful for every day.

Offer Thanks: Offer your appreciation with others through cards to say thanks, verbal articulations, or thoughtful gestures.

Careful Appreciation: Pause for a minute to relish and completely value positive encounters, even little ones.

3. **Taking part in Deep rooted Learning**

Improve mental capability and memory.

Support innovativeness and critical thinking abilities.

Open new open doors for individual and expert development.

Give a feeling of achievement and satisfaction.

Step by step instructions to Embrace Long lasting Learning:

Put forth Learning Objectives: Distinguish areas of interest or abilities you might want to create.

Take Courses: Sign up for on the web or in-person courses, studios, or classes.

Peruse Consistently: Read books, articles, and diaries connected with your inclinations.

Investigate Leisure activities: Seek after side interests and interests that challenge you to learn and develop.

Look for Coaches: Associate with tutors or specialists in your picked field to acquire experiences and direction.

4. **Encouraging Social Associations**
   Decrease sensations of depression and seclusion.
   Offer close to home help during troublesome times.
   Improve sensations of having a place and connectedness.
   Advance sympathy and understanding.
   Step by step instructions to Encourage Social Associations:
   Focus on Connections: Try to keep up with and sustain existing connections.
   Associate with Others: Participate in friendly exercises, clubs, or gatherings lined up with your inclinations.
   Be a Decent Audience: Practice undivided attention while collaborating with others.
   Show Sympathy: Develop compassion and understanding for the encounters and feelings of others.
   Look for Help: Make it a point to out to companions or friends and family when you want backing or somebody to converse with.
5. **Overseeing Pressure Actually**
   Decrease the adverse consequences of constant weight on mental and actual wellbeing.
   Work on your capacity to adapt to testing circumstances.
   Upgrade close to home prosperity and flexibility.
   Instructions to Oversee Pressure Really:
   Profound Relaxing: Practice profound breathing activities to quiet your sensory system and diminish pressure.
   Moderate Muscle Unwinding: Tense and delivery muscle gatherings to ease actual strain.
   Care and Contemplation: Use care strategies to remain present and decrease pressure reactivity.
   Using time productively: Arrange your assignments and focus on liabilities to decrease overpower.
   Put down Stopping points: Lay out solid limits to safeguard your significant investment.
   Look for Help: Make sure to proficient assistance or advising assuming you battle with ongoing pressure or nervousness.
6. **Focusing on Rest**
   Quality rest is fundamental for mental health. During rest, your cerebrum processes feelings, unites recollections, and reestablishes mental capability. Ongoing lack of sleep can prompt temperament aggravations, diminished focus, and expanded pressure.
   The most effective method to Focus on Rest:
   Make a Sleep time Schedule: Lay out a quieting sleep time routine to indicate to your body that now is the right time to rest.
   Limit Screen Time: Stay away from screens (telephones, tablets, PCs) before

bed, as the blue light can upset rest designs.

Establish an Agreeable Rest Climate: Guarantee your room is helpful for rest, with an agreeable sleeping pad and proper room temperature.

Keep a Reliable Rest Timetable: Hit the sack and wake up at similar times every day to control your body's inward clock.

7. **Looking for Proficient Assistance When Required**

   On the off chance that you're battling with relentless emotional wellness issues, looking for proficient assistance is an indication of solidarity, not shortcoming. Advisors, advocates, and specialists are prepared to offer help, direction, and proof based intercessions to work on mental wellbeing.

   Instructions to Look for Proficient Assistance:

   Distinguish Your Requirements: Perceive the signs and side effects of psychological wellness conditions, like tension, gloom, or stress, and connect for help when fundamental.

   Research Experts: Find an emotional well-being proficient who has practical experience in the space of your anxiety, whether it's treatment, directing, or mental treatment.

   Plan an Arrangement: Contact the expert to plan an underlying arrangement and talk about your requirements and objectives.

   Focus on Treatment: Be transparent during your meetings and effectively partake in your treatment plan.

8. **Rehearsing Self-Sympathy**

   Many individuals are their own most brutal pundits. Rehearsing self-sympathy includes treating yourself with the very benevolence and understanding that you would propose to a companion. It can work on confidence, diminish self-analysis, and upgrade generally speaking prosperity.

   Step by step instructions to Practice Self-Sympathy:

   Challenge Self-Decisive Contemplations: When you notice self-decisive considerations, supplant them with self-sympathetic ones.

   Indulge Yourself Generous: Indulge yourself as you would treat a friend or family member in the midst of trouble.

   Practice Taking care of oneself: Focus on taking care of oneself exercises that support your physical, close to home, and mental prosperity.

   Embrace Defect: Acknowledge that no one is great, and it's alright to commit errors and have imperfections.

9. **Embrace Careful Advanced Utilization**

   The advanced age has brought endless advantages yet in addition challenges for mental wellbeing. Inordinate screen time, web-based entertainment correlation, and data over-burden can adversely affect your emotional well-being. Embracing careful computerized utilization includes being deliberate about your internet based exercises and defining sound limits.

   Step by step instructions to Embrace Careful Computerized Utilization:

Routinely Evaluate Computerized Propensities: Think about your advanced propensities and consider whether they are improving or reducing your psychological prosperity.

Put forth Screen Courses of events: Lay out limits on screen time, particularly before sleep time, to advance better rest and diminish computerized related pressure.

Focus on Eye to eye Communication: Really try to associate with others face to face and assemble significant connections past advanced stages.

10. **Participating in Imaginative Outlets**

Participating in imaginative exercises is a superb method for supporting your brain. Whether it's painting, composing, music, or some other type of articulation, innovative outlets can diminish pressure, support state of mind, and advance a feeling of achievement.

The most effective method to Participate in Imaginative Outlets:

Find Your Innovative Enthusiasm: Investigate inventive exercises that impact you and give you pleasure.

Set aside a few minutes for Imagination: Devote time in your timetable for imaginative pursuits.

Embrace the Cycle: Spotlight on the course of creation as opposed to the final product, and don't be excessively disparaging of your work.

The Excursion to Mental Wellbeing

Sustaining your brain is a continuous excursion, not an objective. It includes ordinary practice, self-reflection, and the eagerness to adjust and develop. Recall that psychological health is a powerful cycle, and it's OK to look for help and backing when required.

As you set out on your excursion towards mental wellbeing, you'll probably find that it upgrades your own life as well as emphatically impacts the existences of people around you. Mental health is definitely not a lone undertaking; it swells outward, making a more sympathetic and compassionate reality where people are better prepared to help each other's prosperity.

2.1 **The Mind-Body Connection**

The idea of the psyche body association is definitely not another one; it has been talked about and investigated for a really long time in different societies and philosophical practices. This perplexing connection between our psychological and actual states has significant ramifications for our general wellbeing and prosperity. In this article, we will dive into the psyche body association, investigating its systems, influence on wellbeing, and ways of saddling its true capacity for more noteworthy prosperity.

Understanding the Psyche Body Association

At its center, the brain body association alludes to the complicated transaction between our viewpoints, feelings, convictions, and perspectives (the psyche) and our actual wellbeing and prosperity (the body). It includes the possibility that our psychological and close to home states can impact our actual wellbeing as well as the other way around.

This association is a two-way road, implying that our considerations and feelings can influence our actual wellbeing, and our actual wellbeing can impact our psychological and profound prosperity. A unique relationship highlights the all encompassing nature of people.

The Science Behind the Association

Logical exploration has given significant proof of the brain body association, revealing insight into the physiological components that connect our psychological and profound states with our actual wellbeing. One of the central members in this association is the sensory system.

Autonomic Sensory system (ANS): The ANS is liable for controlling compulsory physical processes, for example, pulse, absorption, and respiratory rate. It is partitioned into two branches: the thoughtful sensory system (SNS) and the parasympathetic sensory system (PNS). The SNS is frequently connected with the "survival" reaction, set off by pressure and gloomy feelings. Then again, the PNS advances unwinding and recuperation. Uneven characters between these two frameworks can essentially affect actual wellbeing.

Chemicals: The psyche body association likewise includes the arrival of chemicals in light of profound states. For instance, stress and nervousness can set off the arrival of cortisol, a chemical that, when persistently raised, can add to different medical problems, for example, hypertension, resistant framework concealment, and weight gain.

The Cerebrum Stomach Hub: Arising research has featured the association between the mind and the stomach, known as the mind stomach hub. This bidirectional correspondence framework assumes a critical part in controlling mind-set, feelings, and gastrointestinal capability. Disturbances in this hub have been connected to conditions like peevish entrail condition (IBS) and state of mind issues.

Psychoneuroimmunology (PNI): PNI is a field of study that investigates the cooperations between the sensory system, the endocrine framework, and the invulnerable framework. Research in this field has demonstrated the way that mental elements, including pressure and close to home states, can impact resistant capability. Ongoing pressure, for example, can debilitate the invulnerable framework's capacity to guard against diseases.

Influence on Actual Wellbeing

Cardiovascular Wellbeing: Ongoing pressure and gloomy feelings have been connected to an expanded gamble of coronary illness. The steady initiation of the thoughtful sensory system can prompt hypertension, irritation, and atherosclerosis.

Insusceptible Capability: Mental pressure can debilitate the safe framework, making the body more powerless to contaminations and illnesses.

Torment Discernment: The brain can impact the view of agony. Pessimistic feelings and stress can compound agony, while good feelings and unwinding procedures can mitigate it.

Gastrointestinal Problems: Conditions like IBS and incendiary entrail sickness (IBD) are frequently exacerbated by pressure and close to home variables, featuring the association between the psyche and stomach wellbeing.

Immune system Illnesses: The psyche body association might assume a part in the turn of events and compounding of immune system sicknesses like rheumatoid joint pain and lupus. Stress can set off or deteriorate immune system eruptions.

Bridling the Psyche Body Association for Prosperity

1. **Care and Contemplation:** Care rehearses, like reflection and profound breathing activities, can assist with quieting the brain, diminish pressure, and advance unwinding. Normal care practice has been displayed to emphatically affect both mental and actual wellbeing.
2. **Mental Conduct Treatment (CBT):** CBT is a remedial methodology that helps people distinguish and change pessimistic idea examples and ways of behaving. It is viable in overseeing conditions like nervousness, sadness, and ongoing agony.
3. **Biofeedback:** Biofeedback procedures permit people to deal with physiological cycles, for example, pulse, muscle strain, and skin temperature. It very well may be utilized to lessen pressure and work on actual wellbeing.
4. **Actual work:** Normal activity has been displayed to emphatically affect emotional wellness by decreasing pressure and delivering endorphins, the body's regular state of mind promoters.
5. **Nourishing Wellbeing:** A fair eating routine wealthy in supplements upholds both mental and actual prosperity. The stomach cerebrum association proposes that stomach wellbeing might impact temperament and psychological well-being, so keeping a solid stomach through dietary decisions is significant.
6. **Rest Cleanliness:** Focusing on quality rest is fundamental for both mental and actual wellbeing. Rest permits the body to rest, recuperate, and control different physiological cycles.
7. **Social Associations:** Building and keeping up with good friendly connections can offer close to home help and decrease sensations of segregation and stress.
8. **Unwinding Strategies:** Consolidating unwinding procedures like moderate muscle unwinding, directed symbolism, and fragrance based treatment can assist with lessening pressure and advance a feeling of prosperity.
9. **Looking for Proficient Assistance:** While managing constant pressure, uneasiness, despondency, or other psychological well-being issues, looking for the direction of emotional well-being experts can be instrumental in working on both mental and actual wellbeing.

2.2 Practices for Mental Clarity

In the present quick moving and data immersed world, mental clearness is a valuable resource. It alludes to the capacity to think obviously, use wise judgment, and keep up with center in the midst of interruptions and mental mess. Accomplishing and supporting mental clearness is fundamental for efficiency, critical thinking, and generally speaking prosperity. In this article, we'll investigate a scope of practices and strategies to help you develop and keep up with mental clearness in your everyday existence.

1. **Care Reflection**
   Diminish Mental Commotion: By noticing your considerations without judgment, you can acquire understanding into your psychological examples and steadily lessen mental prattle.
   Upgrade Concentration: Care contemplation reinforces your ability to support consideration, which is fundamental for mental lucidity.
   Stress Decrease: Rehearsing care can reduce pressure and nervousness, taking into account more prominent mental clearness during testing circumstances.
   The most effective method to Practice Care Reflection:
   Track down a calm and agreeable space.
   Sit or rests with your back straight.
   Shut your eyes and take a couple of full breaths to focus yourself.
   Carry your regard for your breath. Notice the impression of every breath, from the breathe in to the breathe out.
   Assuming your brain meanders, tenderly take your concentration back to your breath without self-analysis.
   Extend your attention to incorporate materially sensations, sounds, and your environmental elements.
   Practice for 10-20 minutes everyday to encounter the full advantages.

2. **Journaling**
   Explain Contemplations: Expounding on your viewpoints and concerns can assist you with seeing them all the more obviously and equitably.
   Critical thinking: Journaling can be a significant device for conceptualizing arrangements and laying out objectives.
   Close to home Delivery: Communicating your feelings in a diary can give help and diminish mental mess.
   The most effective method to Work on Journaling:
   Put away a particular time every day for journaling, whether it's toward the beginning of the, prior day bed, or during breaks.
   Compose unreservedly without stressing over language or design.
   Investigate your contemplations, feelings, and encounters genuinely and truly.
   Think about various journaling procedures, for example, appreciation journaling, continuous flow composing, or objective setting journaling.

3. **Clean up Your Actual Climate**

   Your actual climate can essentially affect your psychological clearness. A jumbled and disordered space can make mental mayhem and ruin center. By cleaning up and sorting out your actual environmental factors, you establish a climate that upholds mental clearness.

   Step by step instructions to Clean up Your Actual Climate:
   Begin with each area in turn, like your work area, storeroom, or parlor.
   Sort things into classes: keep, give, reuse, or dispose of.
   Sort out your excess possessions perfectly, making assigned spaces for every thing.
   Routinely keep up with your cleaned up space to forestall future amassing of messiness.

4. **Focus on and Using time productively**

   Plans for the day: Make day to day or week after week daily agendas to focus on undertakings and keep tabs on your development.
   Time Hindering: Apportion explicit time blocks for centered work, gatherings, and breaks.
   Limit Performing various tasks: Spotlight on each assignment in turn to keep up with mental clearness and efficiency.
   Put down Stopping points: Lay out limits to safeguard your significant investment, both at work and in your own life.

5. **Careful Utilization of Data**

   In the advanced age, we are continually besieged with data from different sources — news, online entertainment, messages, and that's just the beginning. Careful utilization of data includes being purposeful about what you open yourself to and how you draw in with it. This training can forestall data over-burden and mental mess.

   Step by step instructions to Practice Careful Data Utilization:
   Set explicit times for browsing messages and web-based entertainment as opposed to continually looking at over the course of the day.
   Be particular about the wellsprings of data you draw in with, zeroing in on higher standards when in doubt.
   Consider executing computerized detox periods where you disengage from screens and advanced gadgets to intellectually re-energize.

6. **Profound Breathing and Unwinding Strategies**

   Profound breathing and unwinding strategies can rapidly clear your psyche and diminish pressure, upgrading mental lucidity. These practices enact the parasympathetic sensory system, advancing a feeling of quiet and concentration.

   Step by step instructions to Practice Profound Breathing and Unwinding:
   Track down a calm and agreeable spot to sit or rests.
   Shut your eyes and take a sluggish, full breath in through your nose, building

up to four.
Pause your breathing for a count of four.
Breathe out leisurely through your mouth for a count of four.
Rehash this cycle a few times, zeroing in on your breath and relinquishing pressure with every exhalation.
You can likewise investigate other unwinding methods like moderate muscle unwinding or directed symbolism.

7. **Careful Development**

   Actual work, especially careful development rehearses like yoga or kendo, can improve mental lucidity. These practices join actual development with zeroed in consideration on the body and breath, advancing both physical and mental prosperity.

   Instructions to Practice Careful Development:
   Find a tranquil and extensive region where you can move easily.
   Pick a careful development practice that impacts you, like yoga, kendo, or qigong.
   Track with informative recordings or go to classes to learn legitimate procedures.
   Center around your breath and body sensations as you travel through the training.
   Consistently integrate careful development into your daily schedule to encounter its advantages.

8. **Careful Eating**

   The manner in which you eat can likewise impact your psychological lucidity. Careful eating includes focusing on your food, appreciating each nibble, and eating with expectation. This training can assist you with trying not to gorge and upgrade your attention to what food means for your body and psyche.

   Step by step instructions to Practice Careful Eating:
   Establish a quiet eating climate liberated from interruptions like screens or work.
   Pause for a minute to see the value in your dinner outwardly prior to taking a chomp.
   Eat gradually and relish each chomp, focusing on the flavors, surfaces, and sensations.
   Check out your body's craving and totality signals, eating until you are fulfilled instead of excessively full.

9. **Nature and Open air Time**

   Investing energy in nature and open air conditions can significantly affect the brain. Nature gives a chance to detach from advanced interruptions, draw in with the current second, and restore your psychological clearness.

   Step by step instructions to Associate with Nature:
   Go for customary strolls or climbs in regular settings, regardless of whether

they are brief.

Practice open air exercises like planting, setting up camp, or birdwatching.

Dispense time to sit and notice the normal world around you essentially.

10. **Look for Isolation and Quiet**

In our undeniably loud world, looking for snapshots of isolation and quietness can be priceless for mental lucidity. These minutes give space to thoughtfulness, reflection, and re-energizing.

Step by step instructions to Look for Isolation and Quietness:

Commit time every day to be separated from everyone else with your viewpoints, whether it's through contemplation, a performance walk, or just sitting discreetly.

Make a quiet space in your home where you can withdraw for snapshots of isolation and reflection.

Consider infrequent quiet withdraws or nature-based encounters that deal expanded times of quietness.

2.3 Cultivating Mindfulness and Presence

In a world that frequently moves at a frenzied speed, developing care and presence has become progressively significant for our psychological and close to home prosperity. These practices offer a pathway to more noteworthy inward harmony, further developed center, and a more profound feeling of satisfaction. In this article, we'll investigate what care and presence mean, why they matter, and pragmatic ways of integrating them into your life.

Figuring out Care and Presence

Care is the act of paying conscious and non-critical thoughtfulness regarding the current second. It includes noticing your considerations, feelings, substantial sensations, and your general surroundings without endeavoring to change or pass judgment on them. Care supports acknowledgment of the current second for what it's worth, which can prompt decreased pressure and upgraded unwavering focus.

Presence, then again, is the condition completely drew in and submerged in the present time and place. It's described by an increased familiarity with the current second and a profound feeling of association with it. Presence is tied in with being completely present in anything that you are doing, whether it's a basic day to day task or a significant valuable encounter.

Why Care and Presence Matter

1. **Diminished Pressure:** Care and presence can assist you with overseeing pressure by permitting you to answer difficulties all the more handily and with more prominent versatility. You're better ready to deal with tough spots when you're completely mindful of your viewpoints and feelings.
2. **Upgraded Concentration:** Being available works on your focus and mental

capacities. It permits you to connect all the more profoundly with errands and data, prompting better independent direction and critical thinking.
3. **Worked on Close to home Guideline:** Care and presence advance capacity to appreciate individuals on a profound level, assisting you with turning out to be more receptive to your sentiments and those of others. This can prompt better connections and correspondence.
4. **More noteworthy Mindfulness:** These practices support self-reflection and mindfulness, assisting you with figuring out your qualities, needs, and objectives all the more plainly.
5. **More profound Satisfaction:** Presence permits you to relish valuable's encounters all the more completely, prompting a more noteworthy feeling of bliss and satisfaction in regular exercises.

Commonsense Ways Of developing Care and Presence

1. **Begin with Breath Mindfulness**
   Your breath is a strong anchor to the current second. Start by essentially focusing on your breath, seeing its cadence and sensations. Whenever you feel diverted or overpowered, return your concentration to your breath. This straightforward practice should be possible anyplace and whenever.
2. **Careful Eating**
   Eating carefully includes relishing each nibble, focusing on the flavors and surfaces, and eating gradually. Keep away from interruptions like screens or work while eating. Be completely present with your feast, appreciating the sustenance it gives.
3. **Ground Yourself in the Faculties**
   Pause for a minute to completely draw in your faculties. Shut your eyes and pay attention to the sounds around you. Feel the surface of an item, the glow of daylight, or the coolness of a breeze on your skin. Drawing in your faculties carries you into the current second.
4. **Notice Your Contemplations**
   Care includes noticing your contemplations without judgment. At the point when you notice your psyche meandering or hustling, recognize the contemplations and delicately guide your consideration back to the present. This training can assist with decreasing rumination and overthinking.
5. **Practice Careful Relaxing**
   Careful breathing includes deliberately managing your breath to advance unwinding and mindfulness. Attempt the 4-7-8 procedure: breathe in for a count of four, hold for a count of seven, and breathe out for a count of eight. Rehash this example a few times to focus yourself.
6. **Take part in Careful Strolling**

Strolling can be a superb chance to develop presence. Focus on each step, the vibe of your feet contacting the ground, and the development of your body. Strolling carefully should be possible inside or outside.

7. **Set Deliberate Stops**
Over the course of your day, deliberately stop for a couple of seconds of care. These stops can be basically as brief as a little while. During these breaks, shut your eyes, take a couple of full breaths, and focus yourself right now.

8. **Practice Appreciation**
Developing appreciation is a type of care that includes valuing the current second. Every day, pause for a minute to consider things you're thankful for. It very well may be pretty much as basic as the glow of the sun or the grin of a friend or family member.

9. **Make a Careful Morning Schedule**
Begin your day with goal by making a careful morning schedule. This could incorporate contemplation, delicate stretches, or basically partaking in some tea or espresso peacefully. Establishing an uplifting vibe in the first part of the day can impact your outlook for the afternoon.

10. **Embrace Careful Tuning in**
During discussions, practice careful tuning in by concentrating entirely on the speaker. Try not to hinder or framing decisions. Be completely present and participated in the trade, which can prompt better comprehension and association with others.

11. **Ponder Consistently**
Contemplation is an organized method for developing care and presence. Put away devoted time for contemplation every day. There are different contemplation methods, so investigate various styles to find one that impacts you. Directed reflections and contemplation applications can be useful for fledglings.

12. **Embrace Nature**
Investing energy in nature normally cultivates presence. Whether you're climbing in the mountains, walking around a recreation area, or essentially sitting in your lawn, permit yourself to submerge in the normal world around you completely.

13. **Make Careful Minutes in Routine Exercises**
Transform routine exercises into amazing open doors for care. This could incorporate washing dishes, cleaning your teeth, or scrubbing down. Focus on the sensations and developments associated with these errands, changing them into careful ceremonies.

14. **Underscore Better standards when in doubt**
In a world that frequently esteems efficiency and performing various tasks, focus on the nature of your encounters over the amount. Enjoy minutes, connect profoundly, and relish the extravagance of the present.

15. Acknowledge Flaw

Care and presence additionally include tolerating flaw. Having snapshots of interruption or forgetfulness is OK. Rather than condemning yourself, tenderly aide your consideration back to the present with sympathy.

Chapter 3

Fueling Your Body

In this present reality where the speed of life is quick and data about sustenance is bountiful, it very well may be trying to pursue informed decisions about what to ideally eat to fuel our bodies. Nourishment assumes a critical part in our general wellbeing and prosperity, influencing our actual wellbeing as well as our psychological and close to home states. This exhaustive aide will investigate the essentials of nourishment, the significance of a reasonable eating regimen, and useful techniques for pursuing nutritious decisions to fuel your body for ideal wellbeing.

Grasping the Rudiments of Nourishment

Sustenance is the study of how our bodies acquire and utilize the fundamental supplements required for development, advancement, and in general wellbeing. Understanding the fundamentals of nourishment is the most important move toward settling on informed dietary decisions.

1.1 Fundamental Supplements

Starches: These are the body's essential wellspring of energy, found in food varieties like grains, organic products, vegetables, and vegetables.

Proteins: Proteins are fundamental for tissue fix, insusceptible capability, and the development of catalysts and chemicals. Sources incorporate meat, poultry, fish, dairy items, and plant-based sources like beans and tofu.

Fats: Fats give long haul energy capacity, protection, and backing for the retention of fat-dissolvable nutrients. Solid sources incorporate nuts, seeds, avocados, and olive oil.

Nutrients: These are natural mixtures that assume different parts in regularphysical processes. They are gotten through a different eating routine and are tracked down in organic products, vegetables, and braced food sources.

Minerals: Minerals are inorganic supplements fundamental for different physical processes, for example, calcium for bone wellbeing and iron for oxygen transport. Sources incorporate dairy items, salad greens, and lean meats.

Water: Water is fundamental for essentially every normal physical process, including absorption, temperature guideline, and waste expulsion. Remaining hydrated is vital for in general wellbeing.

1.2 Macronutrients versus Micronutrients

Macronutrients (sugars, proteins, and fats) give energy and are expected in bigger amounts in the eating regimen.

Micronutrients (nutrients and minerals) are required in more modest amounts yet are fundamental for different physiological cycles.

1.3 Calories and Energy Equilibrium

Calories are a proportion of the energy given by food and drinks. To keep a solid weight, it's fundamental for balance the quantity of calories consumed with the quantity of calories consumed active work. An overabundance of calories can prompt weight gain, while a shortage can bring about weight reduction.

1.4 Dietary Rules and Proposals

Adjusting Macronutrients: An eating regimen that incorporates an equilibrium of carbs, proteins, and fats.

Eating Entire Food varieties: Picking entire, natural food sources over exceptionally handled choices.

Restricting Added Sugars: Diminishing the utilization of food varieties and drinks high in added sugars.

Watching Sodium Admission: Checking salt admission, which can add to hypertension.

Building a Decent Eating regimen

A fair eating regimen is critical to getting every one of the fundamental supplements your body needs to ideally work. It includes devouring various food sources from various nutrition types to guarantee you get many supplements.

2.1 The Nutritional categories

Natural products: Plentiful in nutrients, minerals, and dietary fiber, natural products give fundamental supplements while fulfilling your sweet tooth. Expect to consume different vivid organic products everyday.

Vegetables: Vegetables are loaded with nutrients, minerals, fiber, and cancer prevention agents. Incorporate a blend of mixed greens, cruciferous vegetables, and bright choices to expand nourishing advantages.

Grains: Entire grains like earthy colored rice, quinoa, and entire wheat give complex sugars, fiber, nutrients, and minerals. Pick entire grains over refined grains for added sustenance.

Proteins: Protein-rich food sources are fundamental for muscle upkeep and different physical processes. Pick lean protein sources like poultry, fish, lean meats, beans, and tofu.

Dairy or Dairy Choices: Dairy items and braced dairy options give calcium, vitamin D, and protein. Pick low-fat or sans fat choices whenever liked.

Fats: Solid fats, like those tracked down in avocados, nuts, seeds, and olive oil, ought to be important for your eating regimen with some restraint. Limit immersed and trans fats tracked down in handled and broiled food sources.

Desserts and Treats: While it's vital for limit added sugars and profoundly handled food sources, periodic extravagances are alright with some restraint.

2.2 Part Control and Adjusted Dinners

Adjusted dinners normally comprise of a blend of macronutrients: carbs, proteins, and fats. Parts ought to be suitable for your age, orientation, action level, and generally speaking wellbeing objectives. Consider utilizing devices like piece control plates or estimating cups to assist with segment the board.

2.3 Dinner Arranging

Plan your feasts and snacks ahead of time.

Set up a shopping rundown to guarantee you have the vital fixings.

Cook in clusters to have quality feasts promptly accessible during the week.

Be aware of part sizes to abstain from gorging.

2.4 Extraordinary Dietary Contemplations

People with explicit dietary requirements, like veggie lovers, vegetarians, or those with food sensitivities or bigotries, can in any case accomplish a fair eating routine. It might require cautious preparation and choosing fitting substitutes to meet dietary necessities.

Supplement Rich Food varieties for Ideal Wellbeing

To fuel your body for ideal wellbeing, zeroing in on supplement rich foods is significant. These are food varieties that give a high centralization of fundamental supplements while limiting void calories.

3.1 Superfoods

Berries: Blueberries, strawberries, and different berries are plentiful in cancer prevention agents, nutrients, and fiber.

Mixed Greens: Kale, spinach, and Swiss chard are loaded with nutrients, minerals, and phytonutrients.

Greasy Fish: Salmon, mackerel, and sardines give omega-3 unsaturated fats and excellent protein.

Nuts and Seeds: Almonds, pecans, chia seeds, and flaxseeds offer sound fats, fiber, and protein.

Vegetables: Beans, lentils, and chickpeas are superb wellsprings of protein, fiber, and fundamental supplements.

3.2 Hydration

Legitimate hydration is fundamental for in general wellbeing. Water is associated with practically every importantphysical process, including absorption, flow, and temperature guideline. Mean to hydrate everyday, and consider consolidating hydrating food sources like watermelon and cucumbers into your eating routine.

3.3 Entire Grains

Entire grains, like earthy colored rice, quinoa, and oats, are supplement rich options in contrast to refined grains. They give complex carbs, fiber, nutrients, and minerals, making them an important piece of a fair eating routine.

3.4 Lean Proteins
Lean proteins, like skinless poultry, fish, tofu, and vegetables, offer excellent protein without unnecessary immersed fat. Protein is fundamental for muscle support, safe capability, and in general wellbeing.

3.5 Solid Fats
Solid fats, tracked down in avocados, nuts, seeds, and olive oil, are urgent for heart wellbeing and mind capability. They likewise assist the body with engrossing fat-solvent nutrients.

3.6 Dairy or Dairy Options
Dairy items and strengthened dairy options give calcium, vitamin D, and protein. Choose low-fat or sans fat choices to diminish immersed fat admission.

3.7 Bright Vegetables and Natural products
Products of the soil of different varieties are plentiful in nutrients, minerals, fiber, and cancer prevention agents. Integrate a rainbow of produce into your dinners to expand wholesome advantages.

Exceptional Weight control plans and Dietary Limitations
Many individuals follow extraordinary eating regimens or have dietary limitations in light of multiple factors, for example, wellbeing concerns, individual convictions, or moral decisions. Exploring these eating regimens while as yet meeting your healthful needs is fundamental.

4.1 Veggie lover and Vegetarian Diets
Veggie lover and vegetarian counts calories prohibit some or every single creature item. To guarantee you get fundamental supplements like vitamin B12, iron, calcium, and protein, plan feasts that incorporate plant-based wellsprings of these supplements or think about supplements.

4.2 Without gluten Diet
People with celiac infection or non-celiac gluten responsiveness need to keep away from gluten-containing grains like wheat, grain, and rye. Settle on normally without gluten grains like rice, quinoa, and corn, and pick without gluten choices for handled food varieties when essential.

4.3 Low-Carb and Keto Diets
Low-carb and ketogenic abstains from food limit starch consumption and underline fats and proteins. While these eating regimens can be powerful for weight reduction, it's fundamental to pick supplement thick food sources to meet your micronutrient needs.

4.4 Food Sensitivities and Bigotries
On the off chance that you have food sensitivities or bigotries, it's essential to peruse food names cautiously and stay away from the particular allergens or aggravations. Counsel a medical services proficient for direction on dietary other options and enhancements if essential.

4.5 Irregular Fasting

Irregular fasting includes cycling between times of eating and fasting. While it might offer some medical advantages, it's vital for pursue supplement rich food decisions during eating windows to guarantee you meet your wholesome necessities.

Systems for Smart dieting

Keeping a good dieting design requires something beyond knowing what to eat — it likewise includes creating positive propensities and systems to help your nourishing objectives.

5.1 Careful Eating

Careful eating includes giving full consideration to your eating experience. It assists you with enjoying your food, perceive yearning and totality prompts, and foster a sound connection with eating.

Eat gradually and relish each chomp.

Try not to eat before screens or when occupied.

Pay attention to your body's appetite and completion signals.

5.2 Part Control

Controlling part sizes can assist with forestalling indulging and backing weight the executives. Utilize more modest plates, measure parcels, and be aware of serving sizes while eating out.

5.3 Cooking at Home

Cooking at home permits you to have more command over the fixings and cooking techniques. Explore different avenues regarding sound recipes, and include companions or relatives in dinner readiness.

5.4 Perusing Food Names

Understanding food names can assist you with settling on informed decisions. Focus on serving sizes, calorie content, macronutrients, and the fixing list. Limit food sources high in added sugars, immersed fats, and sodium.

5.5 Dinner Arranging and Arrangement

Feast arranging and arrangement can save time, cash, and the pressure of choosing what to eat without a second to spare. Plan adjusted feasts, make a shopping rundown, and cook in groups to have sound choices promptly accessible.

5.6 Eating Carefully in Friendly Circumstances

Eating out or going to get-togethers can present difficulties to good dieting. Pick nutritious choices from the menu, practice segment control, and focus on careful eating even in group environments.

5.7 Remaining Hydrated

Legitimate hydration is fundamental for generally speaking wellbeing. Convey a reusable water bottle, hydrate over the course of the day, and consider hydrating food varieties like products of the soil.

5.8 Taking care of Desires and Close to home Eating

Desires and close to home eating are normal difficulties. Practice mindfulness, distinguish sets off, and foster systems to adapt to feelings without going to food.

Think about looking for help from a specialist or guide in the event that profound eating is a common issue.

Unique Contemplations for Various Life Stages

Healthful necessities change over the course of life, from earliest stages to advanced age. Understanding these distinctions and pursuing fitting dietary decisions is fundamental for by and large wellbeing and prosperity.

6.1 Pregnancy and Breastfeeding

During pregnancy and breastfeeding, a lady's nourishing necessities increment to help the developing child and milk creation. Center around an eating routine wealthy in fundamental supplements like folic corrosive, iron, calcium, and protein. Counsel a medical services supplier for customized direction.

6.2 Babies and Youngsters

Sustenance assumes a pivotal part in the development and improvement of babies and kids. Bosom milk or equation gives fundamental supplements to babies, while more seasoned kids benefit from a decent eating routine that incorporates natural products, vegetables, lean proteins, and entire grains.

6.3 Youth

The high school years are a time of quick development and improvement. Satisfactory nourishment is crucial for help physical, mental, and profound changes. Support good dieting propensities and proposition different supplement thick food varieties.

6.4 Adulthood

In adulthood, keeping a decent eating routine backings generally speaking wellbeing, energy levels, and illness counteraction. Focus on supplement rich food varieties and change calorie admission to match movement levels and metabolic changes.

6.5 More established Grown-ups

As individuals age, their healthful necessities might change because of changes in digestion, hunger, and dietary retention. Center around supplement thick food varieties, and think about supplements whenever suggested by a medical services supplier.

6.6 Games Sustenance

Competitors and truly dynamic people have extraordinary nourishing requirements. Legitimate hydration, satisfactory sugars for energy, and a suitable equilibrium of macronutrients are fundamental for max operation and recuperation.

Tending to Normal Healthful Worries

A few normal wholesome worries and medical issue can influence dietary decisions. It's crucial for address these worries and settle on informed conclusions about your eating routine.

7.1 Weight The board

Keeping a sound weight is significant for generally wellbeing. Offset calorie consumption with active work, practice segment control, and focus on supplement rich food varieties to help weight the board objectives.

7.2 Heart Wellbeing
A heart-solid eating routine can assist with lessening the gamble of cardiovascular illnesses. Center around low-sodium choices, limit immersed and trans fats, and consolidate food sources wealthy in fiber and omega-3 unsaturated fats.

7.3 Diabetes The executives
Diabetes requires cautious administration of glucose levels through diet, prescription, and way of life changes. Screen carb admission, pick entire grains, and focus on lean proteins and non-bland vegetables.

7.4 Gastrointestinal Wellbeing
Gastrointestinal circumstances like peevish entrail condition (IBS) and incendiary gut infection (IBD) may require dietary changes. Counsel a medical services supplier or dietitian for customized suggestions.

7.5 Food Sensitivities and Bigotries
Overseeing food sensitivities and bigotries includes keeping away from explicit allergens or aggravations. Peruse food marks, convey dietary requirements in cafés, and consider without allergen choices.

7.6 Bone Wellbeing
To keep up major areas of strength for with and forestall osteoporosis, consume sufficient calcium and vitamin D. Dairy items, salad greens, and braced food varieties are phenomenal sources.

7.7 Wholesome Enhancements
At times, dietary enhancements might be important to address wholesome issues. Counsel a medical services supplier or dietitian prior to taking enhancements to guarantee they are fitting for your particular conditions.

Remaining Informed and Pursuing Informed Decisions
The field of sustenance is consistently developing, with new examination and proposals arising routinely. Remaining informed and settling on informed decisions is urgent for adjusting to these changes.

8.1 Assessing Nourishment Data
While experiencing nourishment data in the media or on the web, basically assess the source and think about the unique circumstance. Be mindful of sensationalized titles and look for data from legitimate sources.

8.2 Counseling an Enlisted Dietitian
Enlisted dietitians are specialists in nourishment and can give customized direction in view of your particular requirements and objectives. Consider counseling a dietitian for customized nourishment exhortation.

8.3 Constant Learning
Nourishment is a long lasting excursion, and there is something else to learn. Remain inquisitive, investigate new food varieties, cooking methods, and dietary

methodologies, and be available to adjusting your eating regimen depending on the situation.

8.4 Adjusting Delight and Nourishment

Sustenance isn't just about sustenance yet in addition about satisfaction. Find an equilibrium that permits you to enjoy the kinds of food while focusing on in general wellbeing and prosperity.

3.1Holistic Nutrition

Comprehensive sustenance is a groundbreaking way to deal with sustenance that perceives the interconnectedness of the whole self. Dissimilar to customary wholesome practices that emphasis exclusively on actual wellbeing, all encompassing nourishment embraces a more extensive point of view, taking into account profound prosperity, otherworldly satisfaction, and natural concordance. In this article, we will dig into the standards and advantages of all encompassing sustenance and investigate how it can improve generally prosperity.

Standards of Comprehensive Nourishment

1. **Entire Food varieties:** Comprehensive sustenance puts serious areas of strength for an on entire, natural food varieties. These food sources are wealthy in supplements, fiber, and fundamental life energy. Models incorporate new leafy foods, entire grains, vegetables, nuts, and seeds.
2. **Bio-Singularity:** All encompassing sustenance perceives that every individual is special, with unmistakable nourishing requirements impacted by elements like hereditary qualities, way of life, and climate. It focuses on customized dietary suggestions custom-made to a singular's particular prerequisites.
3. **Mind-Body Association:** The psyche body association is a key part of all encompassing nourishment. It recognizes that our psychological and close to home states can significantly influence our actual wellbeing. Rehearses like careful eating and stress the board are essential to all encompassing sustenance.
4. **Supplement Thickness:** All encompassing sustenance empowers the utilization of supplement thick food sources that give fundamental nutrients, minerals, and cancer prevention agents. Supplement thick food sources sustain the body as well as help its regular mending and regenerative cycles.
5. **Equilibrium and Control:** All encompassing sustenance advances a reasonable and moderate way to deal with eating. It deters outrageous weight control plans or prohibitive eating designs and supports a sound connection with food.
6. **Supportability:** Natural maintainability is a guiding principle of all encompassing sustenance. It empowers decisions that limit damage to the planet, for example, supporting natural agribusiness, decreasing food squander, and picking privately obtained food varieties.
7. **Careful Eating:** Careful eating is a foundation of comprehensive nourishment. It includes giving full consideration to the eating experience, appreciating each

chomp, and being receptive to craving and completion signals. This training cultivates a more profound association with food and upgrades processing.

Advantages of Comprehensive Sustenance

1. **Worked on Actual Wellbeing:** All encompassing nourishment gives the body fundamental supplements expected for ideal actual working. It can assist with forestalling ongoing infections, improve resistant capability, and advance generally speaking prosperity.
2. **Close to home Equilibrium:** By tending to the brain body association, all encompassing sustenance can work on profound equilibrium and emotional wellness. Appropriate nourishment can uphold state of mind dependability and lessen the gamble of conditions like melancholy and uneasiness.
3. **Expanded Energy:** Supplement thick food sources give supported energy, decreasing the requirement for energy-depleting energizers like caffeine and sugar. All encompassing nourishment can prompt expanded essentialness and endurance.
4. **Weight The executives:** All encompassing nourishment elevates a reasonable way to deal with eating, making it successful for weight the board. It accentuates feeding the body instead of prohibitive eating less junk food, prompting reasonable, long haul results.
5. **Upgraded Assimilation:** Careful eating and the utilization of entire, natural food sources can further develop processing. All encompassing sustenance resolves normal stomach related issues like bulging, heartburn, and blockage.
6. **More noteworthy Mindfulness:** Comprehensive sustenance energizes mindfulness and a more profound comprehension of the body's signs and needs. It cultivates a careful relationship with food, lessening profound and thoughtless eating.
7. **Profound Association:** For a huge number of comprehensive sustenance, the dietary decisions they make are profoundly associated with their otherworldly convictions. This arrangement with one's qualities can prompt a feeling of otherworldly satisfaction and reason.

Step by step instructions to Embrace All encompassing Nourishment

1. **Entire Food sources:** Shift your concentration toward entire, natural food sources. Integrate various natural products, vegetables, entire grains, lean proteins, nuts, and seeds into your eating routine. Limit handled and profoundly refined food varieties.
2. **Careful Eating:** Practice careful eating by giving full consideration to your

feasts. Stay away from interruptions like TV or screens, and relish each chomp. Pay attention to your body's appetite and completion signs.
3. **Customized Sustenance:** Perceive your profile singularity. Your dietary requirements might vary from those of others. Consider counseling a comprehensive nutritionist or dietitian to make a customized sustenance plan.
4. **Profound Prosperity:** Recognize the association between your feelings and dietary patterns. Practice pressure decrease strategies like reflection, yoga, or profound breathing to cultivate close to home equilibrium.
5. **Manageability:** Pursue naturally cognizant food decisions. Support neighborhood and natural farming, decrease food squander, and pick food sources with insignificant ecological effect.
6. **All encompassing Way of life:** Comprehensive nourishment is essential for a more extensive comprehensive way of life. Consider integrating rehearses like standard actual work, quality rest, and profound prosperity into your everyday daily schedule.
7. **Instruct Yourself:** Keep finding out about all encompassing sustenance. Remain informed about the most recent exploration and improvements in the field. Understanding books, going to courses, and investigating legitimate sites can grow your insight.
8. **Stand by listening to Your Body:** Focus on how your body answers various food varieties. Notice how explicit food sources cause you to feel actually, intellectually, and inwardly. Utilize this criticism to refine your dietary decisions.
9. **Look for Help:** In the event that you have explicit wellbeing concerns or dietary limitations, look for direction from a medical services proficient or all encompassing nutritionist. They can give master counsel customized to your requirements.
10. **Practice Persistence:** Embracing comprehensive nourishment is an excursion, not an objective. Show restraint toward yourself as you make changes to your dietary propensities. Progress might come step by step, however the drawn out benefits merit the work.

3.2 The Role of Exercise

Practice is a principal mainstay of a solid way of life, assuming a significant part in advancing both physical and mental prosperity. An incredible asset can work on actual wellness, improve psychological well-being, and add to a greater of life. In this far reaching investigation, we will dig into the complex job of activity, its physical and mental advantages, and functional ways of integrating it into your everyday daily schedule.

Actual Advantages of Activity

1. **Worked on Cardiovascular Wellbeing:** Customary activity reinforces the heart,

diminishes the gamble of coronary illness, and keeps up with solid circulatory strain and cholesterol levels. It additionally improves the proficiency of the cardiovascular framework, permitting the heart to really siphon blood more.
2. **Weight The board:** Exercise assumes a critical part in weight the executives by assisting with consuming calories and fabricate fit muscle. It upholds solid digestion and can support both weight reduction and weight upkeep.
3. **Muscle Strength and Perseverance:** Obstruction preparing and weight-bearing activities increment muscle strength and perseverance. This improves actual execution as well as supports joint security and decreases the gamble of wounds.
4. **Upgraded Adaptability and Equilibrium:** Extending works out, like yoga and Pilates, further develop adaptability and equilibrium. These practices can assist with forestalling falls, lessen the gamble of wounds, and advance in general portability.
5. **Bone Wellbeing:** Weight-bearing activities, like strolling, running, and strength preparing, invigorate bone development and thickness. This is particularly significant in forestalling osteoporosis and keeping up with bone wellbeing as we age.
6. **Improved Invulnerable Capability:** Customary activity can support the resistant framework, making it more successful at warding off contaminations and diseases. It lessens the gamble of persistent infections and supports generally speaking safe wellbeing.
7. **Better Rest:** Exercise advances peaceful rest by directing rest examples and diminishing the side effects of rest issues. It can likewise mitigate pressure and tension, which frequently disturb rest.
8. **Expanded Energy:** Taking part in normal actual work increments energy levels by working on the conveyance of oxygen and supplements to the cells. This outcomes in expanded endurance and decreased weariness.
9. **The executives of Constant Circumstances:** Exercise can be an indispensable piece of overseeing persistent circumstances like diabetes, joint inflammation, and ongoing torment. It can assist with controlling side effects and work on generally personal satisfaction.
10. **Life span:** Concentrates reliably show that customary activity is related with expanded future. It upholds generally speaking wellbeing and prosperity, diminishing the gamble of sudden passing.

Mental and Profound Advantages of Activity

1. **Stress Decrease:** Actual work sets off the arrival of endorphins, frequently alluded to as "inspirational" chemicals. These normal state of mind lifters diminish pressure, nervousness, and gloom.

2. **Further developed Temperament:** Exercise has been displayed to lighten side effects of sadness and tension. It advances the arrival of synapses like serotonin and dopamine, which are related with further developed state of mind and close to home prosperity.
3. **Mental Capability:** Ordinary activity upgrades mental capability, including memory, consideration, and critical abilities to think. It upholds mind well-being by advancing brain adaptability and decreasing the gamble of mental degradation as we age.
4. **Upgraded Confidence:** Accomplishing wellness objectives and encountering actual enhancements can support confidence and self-assurance. Practice gives a feeling of achievement and strengthening.
5. **Better Rest Quality:** Exercise can work on the quality and length of rest. It controls circadian rhythms and diminishes a sleeping disorder, prompting more supportive rest.
6. **Stress Flexibility:** Standard activity upgrades the body's capacity to adapt to pressure by decreasing the physiological reaction to stressors. It cultivates flexibility and close to home prosperity.
7. **Social Association:** Gathering wellness classes, group activities, and outside exercises give valuable open doors to social collaboration and association. These social bonds add to worked on psychological wellness.
8. **Upgraded Inventiveness:** Active work has been connected to expanded imagination and critical abilities to think. It can act as a wellspring of motivation and mental clearness.
9. **Profound Guideline:** Exercise gives a solid outlet to handling and controlling feelings. It can assist with overseeing outrage, dissatisfaction, and profound awkward nature.
10. **Care and Presence:** Exercises like yoga and jujitsu advance care and presence by empowering people to be completely participated in the current second. These practices decrease rumination and advance mental clearness.

Commonsense Ways to integrate Exercise

1. **Pick Exercises You Appreciate:** Find proactive tasks that you truly appreciate. Whether it's moving, climbing, swimming, or playing a game, the more you appreciate it, the more probable you are to stay with it.
2. **Put forth Sensible Objectives:** Put forth reachable wellness objectives that line up with your capacities and inclinations. Continuous advancement is critical to supporting a drawn out work-out daily schedule.
3. **Make a Daily practice:** Lay out a normal work-out schedule that incorporates different exercises. Consistency is critical for receiving the full rewards of activity.

4. **Stir It Up:** Integrate a blend of cardiovascular activity, strength preparing, adaptability, and equilibrium practices into your daily schedule. Assortment forestalls fatigue as well as guarantees extensive wellness.
5. **Find an Activity Accomplice:** Practicing with a companion or accomplice can make exercises more pleasant and give shared inspiration and responsibility.
6. **Use Innovation:** Wellness applications, movement trackers, and online exercise recordings can give direction and inspiration. They likewise assist you with keeping tabs on your development and put forth objectives.
7. **Make It Helpful:** Pick exercises that are open and advantageous for your way of life. Whether it's home exercises, open air exercises, or rec center meetings, make it simple to squeeze practice into your day.
8. **Focus on Recuperation:** Permit your body time to recuperate by integrating rest days into your daily practice. Recuperation is fundamental for forestalling burnout and wounds.
9. **Stand by listening to Your Body:** Focus on your body's signs. On the off chance that you experience torment, uneasiness, or over the top exhaustion, changing your work-out everyday practice or look for direction from a medical services professional is fundamental.
10. **Observe Accomplishments:** Commend your advancement and accomplishments, regardless of how little. Perceiving your triumphs can help inspiration and fearlessness.

3.3 Rest and Sleep for Vitality

Rest and rest are fundamental parts of a sound and energetic life. They assume a critical part in keeping up with physical, mental, and close to home prosperity, and their effect on generally essentialness couldn't possibly be more significant. In this far reaching investigation, we will dive into the meaning of rest and rest, their significant impacts on wellbeing, and commonsense procedures to work on the nature of your supportive rest.

The Significance of Rest and Rest

Rest and rest are not simply times of latency; they are dynamic cycles during which the body goes through fundamental fix and revival. Consider the accompanying key motivations behind why rest and rest are essential for imperativeness:

1. **Actual Recuperation:** During rest and rest, the body completes basic fix processes. This incorporates muscle tissue fix, cell recovery, and the arrival of development chemicals. Sufficient rest upholds the recuperating of wounds and assists the body with recuperating from actual pressure.
2. **Mental Lucidity:** Quality rest and rest are fundamental for mental capability. Rest assumes a urgent part in memory combination, critical thinking,

imagination, and generally smartness. Absence of rest can hinder independent direction and mental execution.
3. **Close to home Prosperity:** Rest and rest straightforwardly affect profound soundness. Adequate rest directs state of mind and close to home reactions, diminishing the gamble of temperament issues like despondency and nervousness. It likewise upgrades profound strength and survival techniques.
4. **Resistant Capability:** Supportive rest is connected to a powerful invulnerable framework. During profound rest, the body produces safe helping substances like cytokines and antibodies. Predictable rest upholds the body's capacity to safeguard against contaminations and ailments.
5. **Actual Wellbeing:** Quality rest is related with a lower hazard of constant ailments, including coronary illness, diabetes, heftiness, and hypertension. Rest and rest add to a decent digestion, chemical guideline, and generally actual wellbeing.
6. **Stress Decrease:** Satisfactory rest and rest assume a critical part in pressure the board. They assist with diminishing pressure chemical levels, advance unwinding, and work on the body's capacity to adapt to stressors.
7. **Life span:** Exploration proposes that people who reliably get quality rest will generally live longer and partake in a more excellent of life as they age.

Understanding the Rest Cycle
Non-REM Rest Stages 1 and 2: These underlying phases of rest are portrayed by light rest, muscle unwinding, and a progressive change into more profound rest. During this stage, the body starts to fix tissues and reestablish energy.

Non-REM Rest Stage 3: Frequently alluded to as profound rest or slow-wave rest, this stage is critical for actual reclamation. It advances muscle development and fix, as well as the arrival of chemicals essential for generally speaking wellbeing.

REM (Fast Eye Development) Rest: REM rest is related with clear dreams and assumes an essential part in mental capability and close to home prosperity. It is the point at which the mind processes and merges recollections, supporting learning and imagination.

The rest cycle ordinarily rehashes on various occasions during the evening, with each total cycle enduring around an hour and a half. An entire night's rest includes different cycles, permitting the body to encounter the full scope of supportive cycles.

Useful Methodologies for Quality Rest and Rest

1. **Focus on Rest Cleanliness:** Lay out a predictable rest plan by hitting the hay and awakening at similar times every day, even on ends of the week. This manages your body's interior clock. Make a quieting sleep time routine to indicate to your body that now is the right time to slow down.

2. **Establish an Agreeable Rest Climate:** Guarantee your rest space is helpful for rest. This incorporates an agreeable sleeping cushion and pads, as well as a cool, dim, and calm room. Consider utilizing power outage shades, earplugs, or a background noise if essential.
3. **Limit Screen Time:** The blue light transmitted by screens (telephones, tablets, PCs, televisions) can disturb rest designs. Stay away from evaluates for basically an hour prior to sleep time. All things considered, take part in loosening up exercises like perusing, delicate extending, or reflection.
4. **Watch Your Eating regimen:** Stay away from weighty feasts, caffeine, and liquor near sleep time. These substances can disrupt rest quality. Pick a light, adjusted nibble if necessary.
5. **Oversee Pressure:** Practice pressure decrease methods like care, profound breathing, or moderate muscle unwinding before sleep time. Journaling or rehearsing appreciation can likewise assist with quieting the psyche.
6. **Remain Dynamic:** Ordinary actual work can further develop rest quality. Hold back nothing 30 minutes of moderate activity most days of the week, however keep away from lively activity near sleep time.
7. **Limit Rests:** While short daytime rests can be reviving, long or unpredictable snoozing during the day can disturb evening rest designs. In the event that you really want to rest, hold it to 20-30 minutes.
8. **Screen Your Rest:** Consider utilizing a rest tracker or diary to screen your rest designs and recognize expected issues. On the off chance that you reliably experience difficulty dozing or experience inordinate daytime weakness, counsel a medical services proficient.
9. **Mind Your Psychological well-being:** Address any hidden emotional wellness concerns, for example, nervousness or sadness, which can adversely affect rest. Talk with an emotional wellness proficient if necessary.
10. **Show restraint:** Quality rest and rest may not work on for the time being. It frequently requires reliable endeavors and way of life changes. Show restraint toward yourself as you work to lay out sound rest propensities.

Chapter 4

Awakening Your Spirit

In the excursion of life, numerous people look for a more profound feeling of direction, association, and satisfaction. This journey frequently prompts the investigation of otherworldliness, a way that goes past the limits of strict doctrine and takes advantage of the embodiment of human life. Otherworldly arousing is the most common way of finding, sustaining, and lining up with one's inward soul, frequently prompting significant self-awareness and a more prominent association with the universe. In this exhaustive investigation, we dig into the multi-layered idea of enlivening your soul, looking at its importance, the ways to profound arousing, and pragmatic strides for sustaining your internal development and association.

Grasping Otherworldliness and Profound Arousing

1.1 Characterizing Otherworldliness

Otherworldliness is a profoundly private and frequently unutterable part of human experience that rises above the material world. It includes looking for importance, reason, and association past the actual domain. While otherworldliness can be communicated through strict practices, it isn't restricted to a specific confidence or conviction framework. All things considered, it includes a wide range of encounters and convictions, from the strict to the mainstream, and from the otherworldly to the philosophical.

1.2 What Is Profound Arousing?

Otherworldly arousing is a significant and extraordinary experience that stirs a person to their real essence and reason. It is portrayed by a change in cognizance, an extended consciousness of the real world, and a profound feeling of interconnectedness with all of presence. Otherworldly arousing frequently includes an uplifted feeling of instinct, sympathy, and a significant inward harmony. It very well may be set off by different life altering situations, including snapshots of emergency, contemplation, or a committed profound practice.

The Meaning of Otherworldly Arousing

2.1 Self-improvement and Self-Revelation

Otherworldly arousing is an excursion of self-revelation. It urges people to investigate their convictions, values, and deepest longings. This course of self-reflection and mindfulness prompts self-improvement, more noteworthy self-acknowledgment, and a more profound comprehension of one's motivation throughout everyday life.

2.2 Association and Solidarity

One of the main parts of profound arousing is the feeling of solidarity and interconnectedness it cultivates. People frequently experience a significant association with different creatures, nature, and the universe overall. This feeling of solidarity rises above limits and divisions, advancing sympathy, compassion, and a more noteworthy worry for the prosperity of every living thing.

2.3 Internal Harmony and Happiness

Otherworldly arousing frequently prompts a condition of internal harmony and happiness. As people line up with their actual selves and let go of connections and inner self driven wants, they experience a profound feeling of serenity and acknowledgment. This internal harmony can assist people with exploring life's difficulties with beauty and strength.

2.4 Extended Awareness and Experiences

Arousing your soul can extend your cognizance and give significant experiences into the idea of the real world. It can prompt a more profound comprehension of the secrets of life, passing, and the universe. These bits of knowledge can significantly influence a singular's viewpoint on presence.

Ways to Profound Arousing

3.1 Contemplation and Care

Contemplation and care rehearses are integral assets for otherworldly arousing. They include preparing the brain to be available and engaged, prompting more noteworthy mindfulness and internal harmony. Ordinary reflection practice can work with profound otherworldly encounters and bits of knowledge.

3.2 Nature and Association with the Earth

Interfacing with nature and investing energy in normal settings can be an impetus for profound arousing. Many individuals track down comfort and motivation in the excellence and agreement of the normal world. Nature energizes a feeling of solidarity and wonderment that can prompt significant otherworldly encounters.

3.3 Yoga and Body-Psyche Practices

Yoga, kendo, and other body-mind rehearses consolidate actual development with care and breath mindfulness. These practices can assist people with associating with their bodies, discharge strain, and access further conditions of cognizance, working with otherworldly development.

3.4 Sacrosanct Customs and Services

Taking part in holy customs and functions, whether as a component of a strict practice or an individual practice, can be an extraordinary encounter. These customs give a feeling of holiness and association that can prompt otherworldly arousing.

3.5 Supernatural and Brushes with death

Supernatural encounters, frequently portrayed as snapshots of direct fellowship with the heavenly or the extraordinary, can set off profound arousing. Brushes with death, in which people report significant experiences with eternity or higher domains, can likewise prompt huge profound change.

Pragmatic Strides for Sustaining Your Inward Development

4.1 Developing Mindfulness

Mindfulness is a foundation of otherworldly arousing. Start by investigating your convictions, values, and inspirations. Journaling, contemplation, and treatment can be important devices for acquiring understanding into your internal world.

4.2 Contemplation and Care Practices

Consider integrating contemplation and care rehearses into your day to day daily schedule. Begin with short meetings and continuously increment the term as you become more agreeable. These practices can assist with calming the brain and work with profound bits of knowledge.

4.3 Associating with Nature

Invest energy in normal settings and develop a profound association with the Earth. Practice careful strolls in the forest, ponder outside, or essentially sit peacefully while valuing the excellence of nature.

4.4 Looking for Direction and Local area

Investigate otherworldly writing, lessons, and customs that impact you. Look for direction from otherworldly guides, instructors, or similar people who can uphold your excursion. Joining a profound local area or gathering can give significant friendship on the way to arousing.

4.5 Rehearsing Sympathy and Administration

Take part in thoughtful gestures and administration to other people. Sympathy and unselfishness are fundamental to profound arousing. By zeroing in on the prosperity of others, you can develop a more profound feeling of association and reason.

4.6 Embracing Give up and Giving up

Otherworldly arousing frequently includes giving up self image driven wants and connections. Work on relinquishing the requirement for control and the quest for outside approval. Embrace the possibility that genuine satisfaction comes from the inside.

4.7 Careful Living

Broaden care and presence into all parts of your life. Practice careful eating, careful correspondence, and careful direction. By living right now, you can extend your otherworldly association.

Defeating Difficulties on the Way

5.1 The Self image and Self-Uncertainty

The self image frequently opposes profound development, gripping to old convictions and examples. Self-uncertainty might emerge as you question your own encounters and bits of knowledge. Perceive these difficulties as a feature of the excursion and practice self-empathy.

5.2 Apprehension and Vulnerability

The course of otherworldly arousing can be joined by dread and vulnerability. Anxiety toward the obscure or apprehension about change is normal. Recall that dread is a characteristic reaction to change, and it very well may be an indication of development.

5.3 Exploring Doubt and Analysis

Not every person will comprehend or uphold your otherworldly excursion. You might experience incredulity or analysis from others. Remain consistent with your way and look for help from the individuals who share your profound goals.

5.4 Persistence and Trust*

Profound arousing is a continuous and frequently nonlinear interaction. Show restraint toward yourself and confidence in your inward direction. Try not to rush or constraining profound encounters, as this can block development.

Embracing an Existence of Otherworldly Arousing

6.1 Incorporating Otherworldly Insights*

As you experience otherworldly bits of knowledge and arousing, look to incorporate these encounters into your day to day existence. Apply the insight acquired from your excursion to your connections, work, and day to day choices.

6.2 Developing Appreciation and Joy*

Develop a feeling of appreciation for the endowments of life, both enormous and little. Embrace bliss as a characteristic condition. Offering thanks and encountering satisfaction are strong ways of remaining associated with your internal soul.

6.3 Serving Others and the World*

Stretch out your profound development to serve others and the world. Take part in demonstrations of administration, natural stewardship, and civil rights. Adjust your activities to your otherworldly qualities to have a constructive outcome.

6.4 Embracing the Journey*

Profound arousing isn't an objective yet a continuous excursion. Embrace the way of nonstop development, learning, and revelation. Remain open to new bits of knowledge and encounters, and be responsive to the consistently unfurling shrewdness of your internal soul.

6.5 Discovering a sense of harmony and Fulfillment*

At last, the journey for otherworldly arousing prompts a significant feeling of inward harmony and satisfaction. As you line up with your actual self and interface with the more prominent universe, you experience a feeling of completeness and reason that rises above the difficulties and preliminaries of life.

4.1 Spirituality and Holistic Health

In the journey for by and large prosperity, people are progressively perceiving the significant association among otherworldliness and all encompassing wellbeing. While customary medication will in general zero in on the actual parts of wellbeing, comprehensive wellbeing embraces a more extensive point of view that recognizes the exchange between the whole self. Otherworldliness, a fundamental element of all encompassing wellbeing, assumes a urgent part in sustaining internal development, close to home equilibrium, and a more profound feeling of direction. In this investigation, we dive into the unpredictable connection among otherworldliness and comprehensive wellbeing, analyzing their importance, the manners by which they converge, and pragmatic systems for embracing both on the way to prosperity.

The Quintessence of Otherworldliness

1.1 Characterizing Otherworldliness

Otherworldliness is a profoundly private and multi-layered part of human life that rises above the material world. It includes the investigation of the significant inquiries of life, reason, and the idea of presence. While otherworldliness can be entwined with strict convictions and practices, it stretches out past strict structures and includes different encounters and points of view.

1.2 The Otherworldly Excursion

At its center, otherworldliness is an excursion of self-revelation and inward development. It welcomes people to investigate their internal scenes, develop a more profound comprehension of themselves, and interface with a higher source or extraordinary reality. This excursion frequently includes practices like reflection, care, petition, and consideration, which work with the investigation of the internal identity and the quest for profound understanding.

Comprehensive Wellbeing: Embracing The whole self

2.1 The Comprehensive Wellbeing Approach

Comprehensive wellbeing is an integrative way to deal with prosperity that perceives the interconnectedness of the whole self. It recognizes that wellbeing isn't only the shortfall of illness yet a condition of equilibrium and concordance among these interconnected parts of our being.

2.2 The Elements of Comprehensive Wellbeing

2.2.1 Actual Wellbeing: Actual wellbeing incorporates the body's general condition, including wellness, sustenance, and infection counteraction. It underscores the significance of standard activity, adjusted sustenance, and preventive consideration.

2.2.2 Psychological well-being: Emotional well-being includes personal prosperity, mental capability, and mental flexibility. Rehearses like pressure the board, treatment, and care add to psychological wellness.

2.2.3 Social Wellbeing: Social wellbeing centers around connections and social associations. It perceives the meaning of solid connections, successful correspondence, and a feeling of having a place.

2.2.4 Ecological Wellbeing: Natural wellbeing underlines the effect of the outside climate on prosperity. It supports eco-accommodating practices, maintainability, and association with the regular world.

2.2.5 Otherworldly Wellbeing: Profound wellbeing is the element of comprehensive wellbeing that relates straightforwardly to the spirit and internal development.

It includes investigating one's qualities, convictions, and association with a higher source or reason.

The Interaction Among Otherworldliness and Comprehensive Wellbeing

3.1 Otherworldliness as a Part of All encompassing Wellbeing

Otherworldliness is a basic part of comprehensive wellbeing since it tends to the spirit's requirements and the quest for significance and reason throughout everyday life. At the point when people sustain their profound prosperity, they frequently experience helps that echo through different components of all encompassing wellbeing.

3.2 Close to home Equilibrium and Flexibility

Otherworldliness gives a wellspring of close to home equilibrium and strength. Rehearses like reflection and petitioning heaven can assist people with overseeing pressure, direct feelings, and track down comfort in testing times. This profound balance adds to mental and actual wellbeing.

3.3 Feeling of Direction and Motivation*

Otherworldliness frequently ingrains a significant feeling of direction and inspiration. At the point when people interface with their internal qualities and a higher wellspring of motivation, they are bound to settle on decisions that advance actual wellbeing, mental clearness, and social prosperity.

3.4 Adapting to Sickness and Suffering*

During seasons of sickness or enduring, otherworldliness can give solace and a feeling of greatness. It assists people with exploring the profound and existential difficulties that frequently go with wellbeing emergencies.

3.5 Comprehensive Mending and Wholeness*

The interchange of otherworldliness and all encompassing wellbeing cultivates a feeling of completeness and equilibrium. This comprehensive methodology perceives that genuine mending stretches out past the actual domain and incorporates profound, mental, and otherworldly aspects.

Reasonable Methodologies for Embracing Otherworldliness and Comprehensive Wellbeing

4.1 Developing Profound Practices*

Consider integrating profound practices into your day to day daily schedule. These may incorporate contemplation, supplication, journaling, or care. Explore different avenues regarding different practices to find those that reverberate with your otherworldly excursion.

4.2 Investigating Internal Growth*

Take part in self-reflection and inward development. Pose yourself significant inquiries about your qualities, convictions, and life's motivation. Look for direction from otherworldly tutors or instructors who can uphold your investigation.

4.3 Focusing on Self-Care*

Comprehensive wellbeing requires taking care of oneself in all aspects. Focus on taking care of oneself practices that support your physical, mental, and profound prosperity. Make a reasonable way of life that upholds your general wellbeing.

4.4 Interfacing with a Profound Community*
Consider joining a profound local area or gathering that lines up with your convictions and values. Imparted otherworldly encounters and associations with similar people can improve your profound excursion.

4.5 Rehearsing Mindfulness*
Embrace care as a method for remaining present and mindful in your regular routine. Care can assist you with associating with your internal identity, oversee pressure, and settle on cognizant decisions that help comprehensive wellbeing.

4.6 Looking for Balance*
Make progress toward balance among the elements of comprehensive wellbeing. Focus on your actual wellbeing by eating great, remaining dynamic, and getting sufficient rest. Focus on psychological well-being through pressure the executives and close to home taking care of oneself. Encourage social associations and draw in with your local area. Embrace natural cognizance and supportability.

4.7 Embracing the Journey*
Perceive that both otherworldliness and comprehensive wellbeing are travels as opposed to objections. Embrace the continuous course of self-disclosure, inward

development, and prosperity. Be patient and humane with yourself as you explore the intricacies of life and keep on developing.

4.2 Practices for Spiritual Growth
The excursion of otherworldly development is a profoundly private and extraordinary way that welcomes people to investigate the inward elements of their being, interface with a higher source, and develop a significant feeling of direction and importance throughout everyday life. It is an excursion of self-disclosure, inward insight, and extraordinary understanding. In this investigation, we dig into rehearses for profound development, analyzing their importance, the manners by which they work with internal change, and useful methodologies for embracing them on the way to otherworldly arousing.

Contemplation and Care
1.1 The Force of Contemplation
Contemplation is a basic practice for profound development. It includes the purposeful development of an engaged and calm brain. Through reflection, people can get to more profound conditions of cognizance, foster mindfulness, and associate with their internal identities.

Down to earth Tips:
Track down a tranquil and agreeable space for reflection.
Begin with short meetings and step by step increment the length.
Explore different avenues regarding different reflection methods, like care contemplation, cherishing graciousness reflection, or directed contemplation.

Practice reflection routinely, in a perfect world everyday, to encounter its full advantages.

1.2 Embracing Care

Care is a condition of present-second mindfulness and non-critical perception. It urges people to completely draw in with the present time and place, developing a profound feeling of presence and association with life.

Commonsense Tips:

Practice care in regular exercises, like eating, strolling, or in any event, washing dishes.

Foster a careful breathing work on, zeroing in on every breath as it enters and leaves the body.

Use care to notice considerations, feelings, and sensations without connection or judgment.

Carry care into moving circumstances to improve lucidity and close to home versatility.

Petition and Consideration

2.1 The Craft of Petition

Petitioning heaven is a profound practice that includes correspondence with a higher source, whether it's viewed as a heavenly presence, the universe, or one's internal identity. It is a demonstration of give up, appreciation, and looking for direction or comfort.

Viable Tips:

Make a hallowed space for supplication, liberated from interruptions.

Foster a normal supplication schedule that lines up with your convictions and expectations.

Supplicate from the heart, communicating your most profound longings, concerns, and appreciation.

Practice both quiet and verbal supplications to interface with the heavenly.

2.2 The Profundities of Contemplation*

Thought includes profound reflection and contemplation. It urges people to investigate significant inquiries of presence, reason, and the idea of the real world. Thoughtful practices can prompt extraordinary experiences and profound development.

Useful Hints:

Devote time to scrutinizing rehearses, for example, journaling, philosophical request, or reflection on significant inquiries.

Understand profound or philosophical texts that resound with your excursion and participate in profound reflection on their lessons.

Look for snapshots of calm isolation to permit pondering bits of knowledge to normally arise.

Embrace receptive request, investigating different viewpoints and ways of thinking.

Associating with Nature

3.1 Nature as a Profound Teacher*

Nature has for some time been viewed as a significant profound instructor. Interfacing with the normal world can cultivate a feeling of wonderment, solidarity, and interconnectedness, working with profound development.

Useful Hints:

Invest energy in regular settings, like stops, backwoods, or close to waterways.

Practice nature care by completely captivating your faculties in the regular habitat.

Consider outside exercises like climbing, planting, or essentially sitting in quietness to associate with the rhythms of nature.

Perceive the excellence and shrewdness present in the normal world as your very own impression internal excursion.

Yoga and Body-Psyche Practices

4.1 Yoga as an Otherworldly Path*

Yoga is an all encompassing practice that consolidates actual stances, breath control, and contemplation. It is both an actual activity and a profound way, assisting people with interfacing with their bodies and internal identities.

Down to earth Tips:

Investigate various styles of yoga, like Hatha, Vinyasa, or Kundalini, to find the one that resounds with your otherworldly excursion.

Practice yoga with care, zeroing in on the sensations in your body and the progression of your breath.

Integrate yoga into your everyday daily practice to keep up with actual wellbeing, profound equilibrium, and otherworldly development.

4.2 Jujitsu and Qi Gong*

Yoga and Qi Gong are antiquated Chinese practices that underscore delicate developments, breath control, and energy development. They advance equilibrium, congruity, and a feeling of inward harmony.

Reasonable Tips:

Look for direction from experienced educators to become familiar with the basics of Judo and Qi Gong.

Practice these disciplines routinely to upgrade actual wellbeing and profound prosperity.

Embrace the thoughtful part of Judo and Qi Gong by carrying careful attention to every development.

Develop a feeling of stream and concordance in your training, both genuinely and profoundly.

Administration and Empathy

5.1 Serving Others as an Otherworldly Practice*

Administration to others is a strong otherworldly practice that cultivates a profound feeling of association and reason. Participating in thoughtful gestures and empathy supports the spirit and advances profound development.

Pragmatic Tips:

Recognize amazing open doors for administration locally or volunteer for purposes that reverberate with your qualities.

Move toward administration with a certifiable heart, zeroing in on the prosperity of others as opposed to looking for individual acknowledgment.

Practice irregular thoughtful gestures in your regular routine to develop a sympathetic outlook.

Perceive the interconnectedness of all creatures and the effect of your activities on the aggregate otherworldly excursion.

Embracing Quiet and Isolation

6.1 The Force of Silence*

Quiet is a rich ground for profound development. In the tranquility of quiet, people can get to their inward insight, associate with the heavenly, and experience significant bits of knowledge.

Viable Tips:

Make customary times of quiet in your day to day daily practice, regardless of whether they are brief.

Practice quiet reflection or examination in a devoted space liberated from interruptions.

Invest energy in isolation, permitting your internal voice to arise and direct you on your otherworldly excursion.

Embrace quiet as a wellspring of inward strength, clearness, and serenity.

4.3 Finding Purpose and Connection

In the embroidery of human life, the quest for reason and association is a crucial string that winds through the existences of people across societies and ages. This immortal journey is a significant investigation of the more profound significance of life, our position on the planet, and our associations with others. Finding reason and association isn't just a quest for individual satisfaction yet additionally an excursion that improves the aggregate human experience. In this investigation, we dive into the meaning of finding reason and association, the manners by which they are entwined, and viable procedures for leaving on this extraordinary excursion

The Meaning of Direction

1.1 Characterizing Reason

Object is the directing power that injects existence with importance and heading. It responds to the essential inquiry of "What am I doing here?" and gives a feeling of lucidity and aim in one's activities and decisions. Intention is certainly not a proper objective yet a steadily developing way that unfurls over the long run.

1.2 The Effect of Direction

Having a feeling of direction significantly affects individual prosperity and generally life fulfillment. It energizes inspiration, strength, and an uplifting perspective on life. Individuals with a solid feeling of direction frequently experience more noteworthy satisfaction, diminished pressure, and worked on actual wellbeing.

1.3 Association with Others through Reason

Reason frequently stretches out past the individual and ventures into the domain of association with others. Mutual perspectives and shared objectives can encourage a feeling of having a place and make solid securities among people and inside networks.

The Embodiment of Association

2.1 The Idea of Connection*

Association is a profoundly human encounter that rises above actual nearness. It includes close to home, scholarly, and otherworldly bonds with others. Association can be laid out through shared encounters, sympathy, and the acknowledgment of our normal humankind.

2.2 The Effect of Connection*

Association is a basic human need that significantly impacts mental, profound, and actual prosperity. It diminishes sensations of confinement, dejection, and sadness. Solid social associations are related with expanded joy and life span.

2.3 Reason through Connection*

Association with others frequently assumes an essential part in finding one's motivation. Cooperative endeavors and shared encounters can enlighten individual and aggregate purposes, prompting a more noteworthy feeling of importance and satisfaction.

The Interchange of Direction and Association

3.1 Reason Driven Connections*

Reason driven associations are connections and networks that structure around shared objectives and values. These associations are much of the time profound, significant, and instrumental in accomplishing normal purposes.

3.2 Association Powered Purpose*

Then again, associations with others can touch off or explain one's feeling of direction. Associations, coordinated efforts, and the trading of thoughts can prompt individual and aggregate experiences that shape one's life way.

3.3 The Intensification Effect*

The interchange of direction and association makes an intensification impact, where every component upgrades and enhances the other. A solid feeling of direction develops associations, and significant associations upgrade one's feeling of direction.

Commonsense Techniques for Tracking down Reason and Association

4.1 Pondering Qualities and Passions*

Start by thinking about your qualities, interests, and interests. What exercises or causes line up with your center convictions? What gives you pleasure and satisfaction? Recognizing these components can be a beginning stage for tracking down reason.

4.2 Investigating Different Paths*

Be available to investigating various ways and valuable open doors. Reason and association can be found in unforeseen spots. Take part in assorted encounters and associate with individuals from different foundations and viewpoints.

4.3 Sustaining Existing Relationships*

Reinforce your current connections by putting time and exertion in significant associations. Share your desires, dreams, and objectives with confided in loved ones. Look for help and cooperation in your interests.

4.4 Joining Reason Driven Communities*

Distinguish people group, associations, or gatherings that line up with your qualities and interests. These reason driven networks frequently give a steady climate to both self-awareness and significant associations.

4.5 Embracing Administration and Contribution*

Take part in demonstrations of administration and commitment to your local area or a reason you are energetic about. Offering in return and helping other people can give a significant feeling of motivation and make associations with similar people.

4.6 Rehearsing Care and Presence*

Develop care and presence in your everyday existence. By being completely present in every second, you can extend your associations with others and reveal the wealth of direction that exists in the present time and place.

Conquering Difficulties on the Excursion

5.1 The Quest for Purpose*

The quest for reason can be testing and may include times of vulnerability. Embrace the excursion of investigation, perceiving that intention is certainly not a proper objective however a dynamic and developing cycle.

5.2 Exploring Relationships*

Constructing and keeping up with significant associations can be perplexing. Be ready to explore difficulties, clashes, and changes in your connections while remaining focused on cultivating association.

5.3 Adjusting Self and Others*

Offsetting individual reason with associations with others might require insightful thought and limit setting. It's fundamental to keep an identity while sustaining associations.

Embracing Reason and Association

6.1 Tracking down Fulfillment*

At last, finding reason and association prompts a feeling of satisfaction and completeness. It gives a significant feeling of importance throughout everyday life and enhances the human experience.

6.2 Adding to a More noteworthy Whole*

At the point when people find reason and association, they add to a more noteworthy entire — the aggregate human excursion. Their activities and connections echo through the interconnected embroidery of humankind, making a snare of mutual perspective and significant associations.

6.3 The Continuous Journey*

Recollect that the mission for reason and association is a continuous excursion, not a limited objective. As you keep on investigating, develop, and interface, you add to the consistently advancing story of human life.

Chapter 5

Emotional Wellbeing

Close to home prosperity is a basic part of human wellbeing and satisfaction. It envelops our capacity to comprehend, make due, and express our feelings really, as well as our ability to fabricate good connections, adapt to pressure, and explore life's difficulties with flexibility. In the present speedy and frequently distressing world, the significance of profound prosperity couldn't possibly be more significant. This extensive investigation dives into the multi-layered domain of close to home prosperity, looking at its importance, the variables that impact it, and reasonable techniques for sustaining and keeping a sound profound life.

Characterizing Close to home Prosperity

Profound prosperity, at its center, alludes to the condition of our close to home wellbeing. It involves perceiving, understanding, and dealing with our feelings in a fair and valuable manner. It implies being on top of our sentiments and answering them in manners that advance generally mental and close to home wellbeing. Close to home prosperity isn't about continuously feeling blissful; it's tied in with having the profound abilities and versatility to deal with the high points and low points of life successfully.

The Elements of Close to home Prosperity

Close to home prosperity incorporates different aspects that add to our in general profound wellbeing. These aspects incorporate profound mindfulness, close to home guideline, relational connections, stress the board, and taking care of oneself. Close to home mindfulness includes perceiving and figuring out our own feelings and those of others. Profound guideline is the capacity to deal with our close to home reactions in a solid way. Relational connections center around building and keeping up with positive associations with others, encouraging everyday reassurance and association. Stress the executives includes adapting really to stressors and life's difficulties, limiting their effect on close to home wellbeing. Taking care of oneself is tied in with focusing on practices and exercises that advance profound equilibrium and prosperity.

The Meaning of Close to home Prosperity

Close to home prosperity isn't simply a good to-have; it's a basic part of by and large wellbeing and personal satisfaction. It impacts different parts of our prosperity, including mental wellbeing, actual wellbeing, life fulfillment, and the nature of our connections. Mental wellbeing and versatility are intently attached to profound prosperity. It furnishes us with the devices to adjust to difficulty, recuperate from misfortunes, and keep an uplifting perspective on life, even despite difficulties. Besides, close to home prosperity significantly affects actual wellbeing. Ongoing pressure and gloomy feelings can add to different medical problems, including cardiovascular issues, compromised invulnerable capability, and stomach related messes.

Besides, people with more elevated levels of profound prosperity will generally report more noteworthy life fulfillment, joy, and a feeling of direction. They are better prepared to explore the intricacies of life and experience a higher generally personal satisfaction. Moreover, profound prosperity assumes a huge part in encouraging positive connections. It empowers people to convey really, feel for other people, and assemble compelling profound associations. Solid connections are a foundation of close to home prosperity and add to a satisfying and significant life.

Factors Affecting Profound Prosperity

A few elements impact our profound prosperity, including natural variables, youth encounters, mental examples, social and ecological elements, and way of life decisions. Natural elements, like hereditary qualities and mind science, can impact our inclination to specific personal difficulties or versatility. Youth encounters, including injury, disregard, or an absence of everyday reassurance, can lastingly affect close to home prosperity in adulthood. Mental examples and manners of thinking assume a critical part.

Pessimistic idea designs, like rumination or catastrophizing, can add to close to home misery, while positive reasoning and mental reexamining can upgrade prosperity. Social and natural variables, including social help, connections, and the general climate, shape our profound prosperity. A solid encouraging group of people and a safe, sustaining climate advance profound wellbeing, while social detachment or poisonous connections can make the contrary difference. Way of life decisions, like eating routine, exercise, rest, and substance use, additionally influence close to home prosperity. A sound way of life can add to profound equilibrium, while unfortunate propensities can fuel inner difficulties.

Techniques for Sustaining Profound Prosperity

Sustaining profound prosperity includes taking on different techniques and practices that advance close to home wellbeing. These methodologies envelop profound mindfulness, care, feeling guideline procedures, building flexibility, sustaining connections, stress the executives, taking care of oneself, and looking for proficient help. Profound mindfulness is the underpinning of close to home prosperity. It includes perceiving and understanding our feelings, which can prompt more prominent mindfulness and profound guideline. Care is the act of being completely present at the time, without judgment. It permits us to notice our considerations and feelings without connection, advancing close to home equilibrium and lucidity. Feeling guideline strategies, like profound breathing, moderate muscle unwinding, or mental social treatment, can assist with overseeing extraordinary feelings really. These strategies give apparatuses to adjust profound reactions and forestall close to home overpower. Building versatility is pivotal for close to home prosperity. Versatility includes defining sensible objectives, critical thinking, looking for help when required, and adjusting to misfortune with adaptability and assurance.

Supporting connections is indispensable to profound prosperity. Positive connections offer close to home help and association, assisting us with exploring life's difficulties all the more successfully. Stress the board strategies, for example, using time effectively, work out, unwinding activities, and side interests, can assist with diminishing the effect of weight on close to home wellbeing. Taking care of oneself practices include focusing on self-sustaining exercises that advance close to home equilibrium, for example, defining limits, participating in exercises you appreciate, and setting aside a few minutes for unwinding and revival. Looking for proficient help is fundamental when inner difficulties become overpowering or tenacious. Treatment and directing can give important direction and instruments to dealing with personal hardships, offering a protected and strong space to investigate and address close to home worries.

Developing Positive Feelings

Developing positive feelings is a vital part of close to home prosperity. Positive feelings, like appreciation, bliss, love, and amazement, contribute essentially to our general life fulfillment. Appreciation rehearses, like keeping an appreciation diary or offering thanks to other people, can help positive feelings. These practices shift our concentration toward the positive parts of life, cultivating a feeling of overflow and satisfaction. Rehearsing self-empathy is another fundamental part. Self-empathy includes treating oneself with thoughtfulness and understanding, especially during troublesome times. It energizes self-acknowledgment and taking care of oneself, upgrading close to home prosperity. Taking part in thoughtful gestures toward others, whether through chipping in

or arbitrary thoughtful gestures, helps those getting the consideration as well as raises the provider's close to home prosperity. Thoughtful gestures create positive feelings and encourage a feeling of association and reason.

The ability to understand anyone on a profound level

The capacity to understand people at their core (EQ) is an imperative part of close to home prosperity. It envelops the capacity to perceive, comprehend, make due, and actually use feelings in oneself as well as other people. Creating the ability to appreciate individuals on a profound level includes further developing abilities like sympathy, mindfulness, and viable correspondence. These abilities improve connections, advance close to home wellbeing, and add to in general prosperity.

Conquering Normal Inner Difficulties

Personal difficulties are a characteristic piece of the human experience, and tending to them is significant for profound prosperity. Normal inner difficulties incorporate tension, misery, despondency and misfortune, outrage, and dejection. Overseeing uneasiness might include unwinding procedures, mental social treatment, and way of life changes. Sorrow, described by persevering misery and a deficiency of interest or delight, may require treatment, drug, way of life changes, and social help.

Adapting to sadness and misfortune includes permitting oneself to grieve, looking for help, and tracking down ways of recalling and honor what has been lost. Overseeing outrage requires perceiving triggers, rehearsing unwinding strategies, and creating better ways of communicating and adapt to outrage. Addressing depression might require connecting with others, joining gatherings, or looking for proficient help. Building associations and encouraging a feeling of having a place are fundamental for conquering depression.

Profound Prosperity Across the Life expectancy

Close to home prosperity is a long lasting excursion that develops over the long haul and changes across various phases of life. Advancing profound prosperity in kids and teenagers includes giving a sustaining climate, showing close to home education, and empowering open correspondence. Grown-ups can focus on profound prosperity by rehearsing taking care of oneself, overseeing pressure, looking for treatment when required, and developing positive connections. More seasoned grown-ups can keep up with close to home prosperity by remaining socially dynamic, chasing after leisure activities and interests, and looking for help for age-related difficulties, like misfortune and confinement. Profound prosperity stays important and significant all through the life expectancy, adding to a satisfying and significant life.

5.1 Understanding Emotions

Feelings are a key part of the human experience, molding our insights, activities, and connections. They are the distinctive varieties that paint the material of our lives, advancing our reality with profundity and significance. Understanding feelings isn't simply a key to mindfulness yet additionally a pathway to exploring the intricacies of human communication and self-awareness. In this investigation, we dig into the many-sided universe of feelings, looking at what they are, the way they work, and why they matter.

Characterizing Feelings

Feelings are mind boggling, complex mental states that emerge because of different improvements or circumstances. They include a large number of sentiments, from bliss and love to outrage and trouble, and, surprisingly, more nuanced feelings like jealousy, sentimentality, or wonder. Feelings are not exclusively results of the psyche; they include physiological changes in the body, for example, shifts in perspective rate, breathing, and hormonal movement. These progressions frequently go with close to home encounters and can act as signs of profound excitement.

The Parts of Feelings

1. **Mental Part:** This part includes the psychological part of feelings, including the abstract insight of the inclination and the considerations and convictions that go with it. For instance, feeling dread might imply considerations of risk or danger.
2. **Physiological Part:** Feelings trigger actual reactions in the body. For example, while encountering outrage, the body might answer with expanded pulse, tense muscles, and the arrival of stress chemicals.
3. **Expressive Part:** Feelings frequently manifest ostensibly through looks, non-verbal communication, and vocal prompts. These articulations can pass our profound states on to other people, working with social correspondence.
4. **Conduct Part:** Feelings impact our way of behaving and activities. For example, feeling adoration might prompt demonstrations of friendship and care, while outrage can bring about fierce or protective ways of behaving.

The Capability of Feelings

1. **Correspondence:** Feelings are a principal method of correspondence, permitting us to pass our inward encounters on to other people. They assist us with communicating our necessities, wants, and concerns, cultivating understanding and association.
2. **Variation:** Feelings have advanced as versatile reactions to ecological boosts. For instance, dread assists us with responding to likely dangers, while happiness supports ways of behaving that advance prosperity and social holding.
3. **Direction:** Feelings assume a huge part in navigation. They give important data about our inclinations, values, and needs, directing our decisions and activities.
4. **Social Holding:** Feelings are fundamental for building and keeping up with connections. They empower us to identify with others, share in their encounters, and structure close to home associations.

The Variety of Feelings

The scene of human feelings is extraordinarily different. While certain feelings are all around perceived and experienced across societies, others are affected by individual contrasts, social standards, and individual encounters. For example, joy and trouble are generally grasped feelings, while feelings like fun at others' expense (delight at another's disaster) or saudade (a Portuguese expression for a profound close to home yearning) might be less natural to some. The wealth of feelings adds profundity and subtlety to our close to home lives, permitting us to explore a wide cluster of circumstances and connections.

The capacity to understand individuals at their core

1. **Mindfulness:** Perceiving and figuring out your own feelings and their effect on your viewpoints, ways of behaving, and choices.
2. **Self-Guideline:** Overseeing and tweaking your profound reactions in a sound and useful manner, including overseeing pressure and staying away from rash responses.
3. **Compassion:** Detecting and understanding the feelings of others, which includes viewpoint taking and certified worry for their prosperity.
4. **Interactive abilities:** Exploring social circumstances really, including successful correspondence, compromise, and building positive connections.

The capacity to understand individuals on a deeper level is a significant expertise that can upgrade individual and expert achievement. It permits people to explore social collaborations, fabricate solid connections, and pursue informed choices in light of both their own feelings and the feelings of others.

The Job of Culture in Feelings

Culture assumes a critical part in forming how feelings are communicated, experienced, and comprehended. Various societies might have unmistakable standards and values connected with feelings. For instance, a few societies might energize the open articulation of feelings, while others might stress close to home restriction and control. Social standards can impact the kinds of feelings considered fitting in different circumstances and the manners by which they are communicated. Understanding social contrasts in profound articulation and discernment is urgent for powerful diverse correspondence and relationship-building.

The Effect of Feelings on Wellbeing

Feelings and psychological well-being are firmly entwined. Drawn out or extraordinary pessimistic feelings, like constant pressure, uneasiness, or discouragement, can unfavorably affect actual wellbeing. They have been connected to different medical problems, including cardiovascular issues, compromised resistant capability, stomach related issues, and, surprisingly, ongoing agony. Then again, positive feelings like delight and appreciation have been related with worked on generally wellbeing and life span. Developing profound prosperity through methods like pressure the board, close to home guideline, and care can emphatically affect both mental and actual wellbeing.

Feelings in Self-improvement and Connections

Understanding and dealing with feelings is a fundamental part of self-improvement and solid connections. At the point when people are in contact with their feelings and can communicate them successfully, they are better prepared to convey their requirements and limits. They can explore clashes valuably, assemble solid associations with others, and encourage compassion and understanding. Sincerely wise people will generally have really satisfying and fulfilling connections, as they are sensitive to both their own close to home reactions and those of their accomplices.

5.2 Managing Stress and Anxiety

Stress and uneasiness are normal buddies in the cutting edge world, influencing individuals of any age and foundations. While these feelings are regular reactions to testing circumstances, drawn out or serious pressure and tension can negatively affect mental and actual wellbeing. Luckily, there are successful procedures to oversee and moderate these sentiments, permitting people to lead more adjusted and satisfying lives. In this investigation, we dive into the idea of stress and nervousness, their expected outcomes, and commonsense strategies for overseeing them.

Figuring out Pressure and Nervousness

1. **Stress:** Stress is the body's normal response to an apparent danger or challenge. It sets off the "survival" reaction, a physiological response that readies the body to manage an expected risk. Stress can be intense, like confronting a cutoff time or experiencing an unexpected emergency, or constant, emerging from continuous tensions like business related pressure or monetary concerns.
2. **Uneasiness:** Tension is a more summed up, industrious sensation of disquiet or misgiving about future occasions or vulnerabilities. It frequently includes unnecessary concern and rumination, even without a trace of a quick danger. Tension issues, for example, summed up nervousness jumble (Stray), social uneasiness problem, or frenzy problem, include constant and extreme uneasiness that can altogether influence day to day existence.

The Results of Unmanaged Stress and Uneasiness

1. **Actual Wellbeing:** Constant pressure can prompt a scope of actual medical conditions, including cardiovascular issues, gastrointestinal unsettling influences, debilitated invulnerable capability, and persistent torment. Uneasiness can add to muscle pressure, migraines, and other actual side effects.
2. **Psychological wellness:** Unmanaged uneasiness can prompt wretchedness, substance misuse, and other emotional well-being conditions. It can likewise impede mental capability, making it challenging to think, decide, or recollect data.
3. **Close to home Prosperity:** Tenacious pressure and tension can disintegrate profound prosperity, prompting peevishness, state of mind swings, and a

lessened feeling of delight and satisfaction throughout everyday life. It can strain connections and confine people from social help.

Reasonable Methodologies for Overseeing Pressure and Uneasiness

1. **Care and Unwinding Procedures:** Care rehearses, like contemplation, profound breathing activities, and moderate muscle unwinding, can assist with quieting the brain and decrease physiological pressure reactions. These strategies advance unwinding and profound equilibrium.
2. **Actual work:** Customary active work is a brilliant method for decreasing pressure and uneasiness. Practice discharges endorphins, normal temperament lifters, and can assist with clearing the psyche. Indeed, even a short walk or extending meeting can have an effect.
3. **Sound Way of life Decisions:** Appropriate sustenance, satisfactory rest, and keeping away from exorbitant caffeine and liquor are fundamental for overseeing pressure and uneasiness. These elements can impact temperament, energy levels, and the body's capacity to adapt to pressure.
4. **Using time effectively:** Successful using time productively can diminish pressure connected with work or everyday obligations. Focusing on undertakings, laying out sensible objectives, and breaking projects into reasonable advances can assist with forestalling feeling overpowered.
5. **Mental Conduct Methods:** Mental social treatment (CBT) is a generally involved approach for overseeing uneasiness. It includes distinguishing and testing negative idea examples and creating better perspectives and answering stressors.
6. **Looking for Help:** Conversing with a confided in companion, relative, or specialist can offer close to home help and a point of view beyond your own. Strong connections are fundamental for overseeing pressure and nervousness.
7. **Laying out Limits:** Defining clear limits in both individual and expert life is essential for overseeing pressure. Saying "no" when essential and perceiving your cutoff points can forestall overcommitment and burnout.
8. **Participating in Side interests and Unwinding:** Taking part in side interests, imaginative exercises, and unwinding practices can give a significant getaway from stressors. These exercises advance delight and proposition a reprieve from day to day pressures.
9. **Staying away from Hairsplitting:** Taking a stab at flawlessness can be a huge wellspring of stress and nervousness. Embrace blemish and spotlight on progress as opposed flawlessly in your undertakings.
10. **Proficient Assistance:** Assuming pressure and tension persevere or meddle altogether with day to day existence, it is fundamental for look for proficient

assistance. Specialists and advisors can give custom-made procedures and backing to dealing with these difficulties.

The Job of Way of life in Pressure and Uneasiness The executives

1. **Diet:** A decent eating regimen that incorporates various supplements can uphold by and large wellbeing, including psychological well-being. Certain food varieties, like those
   wealthy in omega-3 unsaturated fats (e.g., greasy fish), cell reinforcements (e.g., products of the soil), and complex carbs (e.g., entire grains), can emphatically affect state of mind and feelings of anxiety.
2. **Rest:** Sufficient and soothing rest is fundamental for profound and mental prosperity. Laying out a steady rest routine and establishing a rest favorable climate can further develop rest quality.
3. **Actual work:** Customary active work lessens pressure as well as further develops state of mind and mental capability. Finding charming proactive tasks can make practice an economical piece of your daily schedule.
4. **Substance Use:** Unreasonable utilization of caffeine, liquor, or sporting medications can compound uneasiness and stress. Lessening or disposing of these substances might emphatically affect emotional well-being.
5. **Social Help:** Keeping up with and sustaining positive associations with loved ones offers close to home help and a feeling of having a place. Social associations are fundamental for overseeing pressure and tension.

5.3 Cultivating Positive Emotions

Positive feelings, like euphoria, appreciation, love, and satisfaction, are short lived snapshots of bliss as well as foundations of a satisfying and significant life. Developing positive feelings isn't just a method for encountering more noteworthy euphoria and prosperity yet additionally a way to construct flexibility, further develop connections, and improve by and large mental and actual wellbeing. In this investigation, we dig into the significance of positive feelings, the science behind them, and reasonable techniques for developing a more good profound scene.

The Significance of Positive Feelings

1. **Worked on Psychological wellness:** Positive feelings have been connected to diminished side effects of melancholy and tension. They go about as supports against pressure and can assist people with adapting to life's difficulties all the more actually.
2. **Upgraded Actual Wellbeing:** Exploration proposes that encountering positive feelings can emphatically affect actual wellbeing. They are related with

lower circulatory strain, worked on invulnerable capability, and diminished irritation.
3. **Versatility:** Positive feelings add to flexibility, assisting people with returning quickly from misfortune and difficulties all the more actually. They give a mental cushion against the adverse consequences of stress.
4. **Mental Advantages:** Positive feelings upgrade mental capability, including imagination, critical thinking, and adaptable reasoning. They expand one's viewpoint and empower investigation and learning.
5. **Social Associations:** Positive feelings are infectious and work with social associations. They advance participation, fortify connections, and encourage a feeling of having a place and local area.

The Study of Positive Feelings

1. **The Expand and-Fabricate Hypothesis:** Created by Barbara Fredrickson, this hypothesis proposes that positive feelings widen a singular's thought-activity collection. While encountering positive feelings, people are bound to investigate additional opportunities, take part in imaginative reasoning, and fabricate important social associations. Over the long haul, this expanding impact constructs assets, for example, strength and social help, that add to long haul prosperity.
2. **The Fixing Speculation:** Positive feelings have the ability to "fix" the physiological impacts of pessimistic feelings and stress. For instance, encountering bliss or chuckling can prompt the unwinding of muscles, decreased pulse, and the arrival of feel-great neurochemicals like endorphins.
3. **The Vertical Twisting:** Taking part in exercises that evoke positive feelings can set off a vertical winding of prosperity. For example, participating in thoughtful gestures can prompt sensations of satisfaction, which, thus, move further thoughtful gestures and positive feelings.

Reasonable Systems for Developing Positive Feelings

1. **Appreciation Practices:** Consistently offering thanks is a strong method for developing positive feelings. Keep an appreciation diary where you record things you are grateful for every day. Offer thanks to others through cards to say thanks or tokens of thoughtfulness.
2. **Care and Present Second Mindfulness:** Care rehearses include being completely present at the time, without judgment. Taking part in care reflection or just enjoying the tactile encounters of day to day existence can expand familiarity with positive minutes.
3. **Thoughtful gestures:** Performing thoughtful gestures toward others benefits

them as well as produces positive feelings in you. Whether it's aiding a companion, chipping in, or offering a thoughtful word to a more peculiar, thoughtful gestures advance sensations of happiness and fulfillment.
4. **Develop Positive Connections:** Building and sustaining positive connections can be a huge wellspring of positive feelings. Invest energy with friends and family, participate in significant discussions, and express warmth and appreciation.
5. **Seek after Stream Exercises:** Stream is a condition of profound commitment and delight in an action. Recognize and participate in exercises that bring you into a stream state, whether it's an imaginative pursuit, a game, or a leisure activity.
6. **Practice Self-Empathy:** Indulge yourself with consideration and self-sympathy. Rather than cruel self-analysis, offer getting it and backing to yourself, especially during troublesome times.
7. **Exquisite Positive Encounters:** Set aside some margin to enjoy and completely experience positive minutes. Whether it's partaking in a delightful feast, savoring a lovely dusk, or valuing a sincere discussion, enjoying escalates the positive feelings related with the experience.
8. **Giggling and Humor:** Chuckling is a characteristic wellspring of satisfaction and prosperity. Take part in exercises that make you giggle, whether it's watching an entertaining film, understanding jokes, or investing energy with comical companions.
9. **Put forth and Accomplish Objectives:** Defining and achieving significant objectives can inspire positive feelings. The feeling of achievement and progress can cultivate a deep satisfaction and fulfillment.
10. **Practice Hopefulness:** Develop a hopeful point of view by zeroing in on certain perspectives and potential outcomes. Challenge negative idea examples and work on rethinking circumstances in a more certain light.

Difficulties and Traps

While developing positive feelings is helpful, it's critical to recognize that life isn't generally a constant stream of good encounters. There will be difficulties, misfortunes, and gloomy feelings. It's pivotal to permit space for the full scope of human feelings and not to stifle or deny gloomy sentiments. All things being equal, the objective is to find

some kind of harmony, perceiving that both positive and gloomy feelings are important for the human experience. Besides, realness in encountering and communicating feelings, both good and pessimistic, is fundamental for close to home prosperity.

Chapter 6

Holistic Healing Therapies

All encompassing recuperating treatments are a different cluster of approaches that mean to regard the person overall, tending to actual sicknesses as well as close to home, mental, and otherworldly prosperity. Established in old customs and current developments, these treatments perceive the interconnectedness of all parts of wellbeing and try to advance equilibrium, congruity, and recuperating in the brain, body, and soul. In this far reaching investigation, we dig into the universe of comprehensive mending treatments, analyzing their standards, rehearses, and the different scope of modalities that fall under this umbrella.

Figuring out All encompassing Recuperating

Comprehensive mending, frequently alluded to as all encompassing medication or reciprocal and elective medication (CAM), is a way of thinking of medical services that thinks about the whole individual — body, psyche, feelings, and soul — chasing wellbeing and health. It depends on the reason that wellbeing isn't simply the shortfall of illness however the presence of equilibrium and imperativeness in all parts of life. All encompassing recuperating perceives that every individual is novel and that the main drivers of disease or awkwardness might shift from one individual to another.

Standards of All encompassing Recuperating

1. **Comprehensive quality:** The center guideline of all encompassing recuperating is comprehensive quality, and that implies seeing the person in general as opposed to an assortment of discrete parts or side effects. This approach accentuates the interconnection between physical, mental, close to home, and profound parts of wellbeing.
2. **Individualization:** All encompassing treatments are custom-made to the singular's one of a kind necessities and conditions. Experts consider the person's

actual wellbeing, profound state, way of life, and individual convictions while fostering a treatment plan.

3. **Counteraction:** All encompassing recuperating puts serious areas of strength for an on counteraction and keeping up with generally speaking wellbeing and prosperity. This
incorporates way of life changes, dietary decisions, and stress the board to forestall ailment before it happens.
4. **Regular Recuperating:** Numerous all encompassing treatments utilize normal cures and medicines, including home grown medication, dietary changes, and exercise based recuperations. The emphasis is on supporting the body's intrinsic mending skills.
5. **Mind-Body-Soul Association:** All encompassing mending recognizes the significant association between the psyche, body, and soul. It perceives that profound and otherworldly prosperity can essentially influence actual wellbeing.
6. **Equilibrium and Amicability:** The objective of all encompassing recuperating is to reestablish harmony and agreement in all parts of life. Irregularity is viewed as a main driver of sickness and infection.

Normal All encompassing Mending Modalities

There is many comprehensive recuperating modalities, each with its own standards and practices. Here are probably the most regularly utilized treatments:

1. Needle therapy: A conventional Chinese medication practice that includes embedding meager needles into explicit focuses on the body to invigorate energy stream (Qi) and advance equilibrium. Needle therapy is utilized for various circumstances, including torment the executives and stress decrease.
2. **Ayurveda:** An old arrangement of medication from India that spotlights on adjusting the body's doshas (Vata, Pitta, Kapha) through diet, way of life, home grown cures, and practices like yoga and contemplation.
3. **Home grown Medication:** The utilization of plants and plant removes for the purpose of mending. Home grown cures are utilized to treat a great many circumstances, from normal colds to constant diseases.
4. **Homeopathy:** An arrangement of medication in light of the guideline of "like fixes like," where profoundly weakened substances that imitate the side effects of a sickness are utilized to invigorate the body's regular mending reaction.
5. **Chiropractic Care:** A medical services discipline that spotlights on the outer muscle framework and its effect on generally wellbeing. Bone and joint specialists utilize spinal changes and controls to treat different medical problems.
6. **Naturopathy:** An all encompassing way to deal with medical care that joins normal treatments, dietary proposals, and way of life changes to advance health and forestall sickness.

7. **Energy Mending:** Treatments like Reiki, Recuperating Contact, and Restorative Touch that include the utilization of energy to adjust and recuperate the body's energy fields.
8. **Mind-Body Practices:** These incorporate contemplation, care, yoga, Judo, and Qigong. These practices advance unwinding, decrease pressure, and improve mental and profound prosperity.
9. **All encompassing Nourishment:** An emphasis on involving food as medication, stressing entire, supplement thick food sources and customized dietary intends to address explicit wellbeing concerns.
10. **Fragrant healing:** The utilization of rejuvenating oils from plants to advance physical, close to home, and profound prosperity. Fragrant healing is in many cases utilized related to knead or as a type of unwinding treatment.
11. **Conventional Recuperating Frameworks:** Native and customary mending frameworks from different societies, like Local American medication, African herbalism, and Australian Native mending rehearses.
12. **Bodywork Treatments:** These incorporate back rub treatment, craniosacral treatment, and reflexology, which control the body's delicate tissues to advance unwinding and recuperating.
13. **Craftsmanship and Music Treatment:** Innovative expressions treatments that utilization creative articulation, like visual expressions or music, to advance profound mending and self-articulation.
14. **All encompassing Psychotherapy:** A helpful methodology that coordinates conventional psychotherapy with comprehensive standards, tending to mental and close to home wellbeing with regards to the entire individual.
15. **Biofeedback:** A method that permits people to deal with physiological capabilities, for example, pulse and muscle pressure, to lessen pressure and work on generally prosperity.

The Comprehensive Recuperating Excursion

Setting out on a comprehensive mending venture frequently includes an all encompassing evaluation, where a professional thinks about different parts of the singular's life, including actual wellbeing, close to home prosperity, way of life, and otherworldly convictions. This evaluation directs the improvement of a customized treatment plan that might incorporate a blend of comprehensive treatments.

All encompassing Recuperating and Traditional Medication

It's fundamental for note that comprehensive mending isn't really a swap for customary medication yet can be utilized related to it. Numerous people decide to coordinate comprehensive treatments into their medical care routine to supplement the therapies recommended by clinical specialists. This integrative methodology is known as reciprocal and elective medication (CAM) and means to give a more extensive and all encompassing way to deal with medical care.

Studies and Discussions

All encompassing mending isn't without its contentions and studies. Some contend that it needs logical meticulousness and depends on narrative proof as opposed to thorough clinical preliminaries. Others are worried about the potential for deception and pseudoscientific practices inside the all encompassing mending local area.

6.1 Complementary and Alternative Medicine

Corresponding and Elective Medication (CAM) envelops a different scope of medical care practices, treatments, and approaches that exist outside the domain of regular Western medication. CAM treatments are frequently utilized close by, or as supplements to, standard clinical medicines. While the viability of some CAM rehearses stays a subject of discussion, others have earned respect for their part in advancing prosperity, overseeing persistent circumstances, and tending to different parts of wellbeing. In this investigation, we dive into the universe of CAM, looking at its standards, famous modalities, and its advancing job in medical services.

Figuring out Correlative and Elective Medication (CAM)

CAM alludes to a general classification of medical care practices and therapies that fall outside the extent of ordinary Western medication. It's fundamental to recognize "reciprocal" and "option" approaches inside CAM:

Reciprocal Medication: Corresponding treatments are utilized close by regular clinical medicines to upgrade their belongings or lighten incidental effects. For instance, a disease patient might utilize needle therapy to oversee chemotherapy-initiated queasiness.

Elective Medication: Elective treatments are utilized instead of ordinary clinical medicines. For this situation, people pick CAM as their essential method of medical services. For example, somebody with constant torment could select chiropractic care rather than remedy torment prescription.

CAM envelops a variety of modalities, going from customary practices attached in old societies to later developments. Some CAM treatments have acquired far reaching acknowledgment, while others stay on the edges of standard medical care.

Famous Modalities inside CAM

CAM treatments are essentially as different as the people who use them. Here are probably the most generally perceived and rehearsed CAM modalities:

1. **Needle therapy:** An old Chinese practice that includes embedding dainty needles into explicit focuses on the body to invigorate energy stream and advance equilibrium. Needle therapy is usually utilized for torment the executives and stress decrease.
2. **Chiropractic Care:** A medical services discipline that spotlights on the outer muscle framework, especially the spine. Alignment specialists utilize spinal changes and controls to treat different circumstances, including back torment and outer muscle issues.

3. **Natural Medication:** The utilization of plants and plant separates for the end goal of recuperating. Home grown cures are utilized to address an extensive variety of wellbeing worries, from normal colds to persistent sicknesses.
4. **Homeopathy:** An arrangement of medication in view of the rule of "like fixes like," where profoundly weakened substances that mirror the side effects of a disease are utilized to invigorate the body's regular mending reaction.
5. **Naturopathy:** A comprehensive way to deal with medical care that consolidates normal treatments, dietary proposals, and way of life changes to advance wellbeing and forestall sickness.
6. **Mind-Body Practices:** These incorporate reflection, care, yoga, Judo, and Qigong. These practices advance unwinding, lessen pressure, and improve mental and profound prosperity.
7. **Energy Recuperating:** Treatments like Reiki, Mending Contact, and Restorative Touch that include the utilization of energy to adjust and recuperate the body's energy fields.
8. **Ayurveda:** An old arrangement of medication from India that spotlights on adjusting the body's doshas (Vata, Pitta, Kapha) through diet, way of life, home grown cures, and practices like yoga and contemplation.
9. **Fragrance based treatment:** The utilization of medicinal balms from plants to advance physical, profound, and otherworldly prosperity. Fragrant healing is in many cases utilized related to rub or as a type of unwinding treatment.
10. **Conventional Recuperating Frameworks:** Native and customary mending frameworks from different societies, like Local American medication, African herbalism, and Australian Native recuperating rehearses.
11. **Biofeedback:** A procedure that permits people to deal with physiological capabilities, for example, pulse and muscle strain, to diminish pressure and work on generally speaking prosperity.
12. **Hypnotherapy:** The utilization of entrancing to initiate a condition of centered consideration and unwinding. Hypnotherapy is utilized for different purposes, including torment the board and changing on a surface level.
13. **Conventional Chinese Medication (TCM):** An old arrangement of medication that incorporates needle therapy, natural medication, dietary treatment, and practices like Yoga and Qi Gong. TCM centers around adjusting the body's indispensable energy (Qi) and Yin-Yang standards.

The Advancing Job of CAM in Medical services

Throughout the course of recent many years, CAM has encountered a critical development in its job inside the medical services scene. A few key improvements include:

1. **Integrative Medication:** Integrative medication addresses a cooperative

methodology that joins customary clinical medicines with proof based CAM treatments. Numerous medical care establishments presently offer integrative medication programs, perceiving the worth of all encompassing consideration.

2. **Exploration and Proof:** As interest in CAM has developed, so has the group of logical examination analyzing the wellbeing and adequacy of different CAM treatments. This examination assists medical services suppliers with settling on educated conclusions about the reconciliation regarding CAM into patient consideration.
3. **Patient-Focused Care:** CAM treatments frequently underline a patient-focused approach, zeroing in on individualized care and patient strengthening. This lines up with the developing pattern in medical services toward customized medication.
4. **All encompassing Health:** CAM advances the idea of comprehensive health, stressing the treatment of infection as well as the anticipation of ailment and the upgrade of generally speaking prosperity. This lines up with a change in medical care toward proactive and preventive methodologies.
5. **Acknowledgment and Guideline:** In certain nations, CAM treatments and specialists are dependent upon guideline and licensure to guarantee wellbeing and nature of care. This acknowledgment has added to more prominent acknowledgment and incorporation of CAM into standard medical services.

Contentions and Studies

Regardless of its developing acknowledgment, CAM isn't without its debates and investigates. A few worries include:

1. **Absence of Guideline:** CAM is a different field, and not all treatments are directed or dependent upon thorough principles. This can prompt fluctuation in the quality and wellbeing of CAM rehearses.
2. **Viability and Wellbeing:** The viability and security of some CAM treatments stay a subject of discussion. Not all CAM rehearses have been exposed to thorough logical investigation, and individual reactions to treatments can change broadly.
3. **Pseudoscience:** Some CAM rehearses are scrutinized for without a logical premise or for advancing pseudoscientific cases. It's fundamental for people to be basic and knowing while investigating CAM choices.
4. **Potential for Mischief:** Like any clinical mediation, CAM treatments can convey chances, particularly when utilized improperly or without legitimate management. People ought to talk with qualified professionals and illuminate their medical care suppliers about any CAM treatments they are utilizing.

6.2 Energy Healing Modalities

Energy recuperating modalities are a different arrangement of practices that work with the idea of essential energy, referred to by different names like Qi (in Chinese), Prana (in Hinduism), or life force energy. These methodologies depend on the possibility that uneven characters or blockages in the progression of this energy can prompt physical, close to home, or otherworldly afflictions. Energy mending looks to reestablish concordance and essentialness by tending to these irregular characteristics. In this investigation, we dig into the universe of energy mending modalities, analyzing their standards, rehearses, and their job in advancing all encompassing prosperity.

Understanding Energy Mending

Energy recuperating is established in the conviction that a hidden energy or daily routine power quickens all experiencing creatures. This energy courses through the body along pathways or channels, and disturbances in this stream can prompt different types of uneasiness, illness, or profound trouble. Energy recuperating modalities mean to recognize and address these blockages or lopsided characteristics to reestablish wellbeing and imperativeness.

While energy mending has old roots in societies around the world, it is frequently seen with suspicion by current Western medication because of the absence of experimental logical proof. Be that as it may, its ubiquity has filled as of late, and numerous people have announced positive encounters and advantages from energy recuperating rehearses.

Standards of Energy Mending

Energy mending modalities are directed by a few key standards:

1. **Imperative Energy:** Integral to energy mending is the idea of crucial energy, frequently alluded to by different names like Qi, Prana, or life force energy. This energy is accepted to move through the body and is fundamental for wellbeing and imperativeness.
2. **Equilibrium and Concordance:** Energy mending looks to reestablish harmony and agreement inside the body, brain, and soul. It tends to the underlying drivers of lopsided characteristics, instead of simply treating side effects.
3. **Comprehensive Viewpoint:** Energy recuperating thinks about the entire individual, including physical, close to home, mental, and profound angles. It perceives that awkward nature in one region can influence the general prosperity of a person.
4. **Self-Mending:** Energy recuperating modalities frequently engage people to partake effectively in their recuperating cycle. Professionals might help clients procedures to work with their own energy, advancing self-mending.

Famous Energy Recuperating Modalities

Energy recuperating incorporates a large number of modalities, each with its own standards and practices. Here are the absolute most broadly perceived and rehearsed energy recuperating modalities:

1. **Reiki:** Reiki is a Japanese recuperating practice that includes the exchange of energy from the professional to the beneficiary through light touch or close body developments. It intends to advance unwinding, decrease pressure, and work with recuperating.
2. **Mending Contact:** Recuperating Contact is a delicate, painless energy treatment that utilizations involved or close body procedures to clear, balance, and blend the human energy framework. It is many times used to diminish agony, nervousness, and stress.
3. **Pranic Recuperating:** Pranic Mending depends on the guideline of purifying and invigorating the body's energy communities, known as chakras. Experts utilize their hands to check and control the energy field to advance mending.
4. **Precious stone Recuperating:** Gem mending includes the utilization of different precious stones and gemstones to adjust and orchestrate energy. Various stones are accepted to have explicit properties and consequences for the energy framework.
5. **Quantum Contact:** Quantum Contact is an involved recuperating strategy that spotlights on breathing and body attention to raise and direct life force energy to advance mending. It is frequently utilized for help with discomfort and close to home prosperity.
6. **Biofield Treatments:** Biofield treatments, like Remedial Touch and Recuperating Contact, include working with the human energy field to work with mending. Experts utilize their hands to control energy stream.
7. **Extremity Treatment:** Extremity Treatment joins bodywork, diet, and exercise with energy adjusting strategies to advance wellbeing and prosperity. It looks to adjust the body's electromagnetic energy.
8. **Pranic Psychotherapy:** A specific type of Pranic Mending, Pranic Psychotherapy centers around the profound and mental parts of wellbeing and prosperity. It means to deliver profound blockages and advance mental lucidity.
9. **Quantum Mending Spellbinding Method (QHHT):** QHHT consolidates entrancing with energy recuperating procedures to access previous existences and the higher self for recuperating and direction.
10. **Sound Mending:** Sound recuperating utilizes different sound devices, like singing dishes, tuning forks, or voice, to impact the body's energy field and advance unwinding and mending.

The Job of Energy Mending in All encompassing Prosperity

Energy mending modalities are frequently incorporated into comprehensive prosperity rehearses that underline the interconnectedness of the body, psyche, and soul.

They can be utilized to help regular clinical medicines or as independent treatments for advancing wellbeing and essentialness. A few people go to energy recuperating for help from actual diseases, inner difficulties, or for of self-improvement and self-revelation.

Scrutinizes and Debates

Energy mending modalities are not without their debates and studies. Doubters contend that the idea of indispensable energy needs logical approval, and the components by which energy mending works remain inadequately comprehended. While certain people report critical advantages from energy recuperating rehearses, others don't encounter similar impacts, prompting differing suppositions on their viability.

6.3 Integrating Holistic Therapies

Coordinating all encompassing treatments into one's medical services routine includes consolidating many correlative and elective practices close by regular clinical therapies. This approach recognizes the interconnectedness of physical, close to home, mental, and otherworldly prosperity, stressing an all encompassing perspective on wellbeing. By mixing both ordinary and all encompassing treatments, people expect to accomplish a thorough way to deal with health, tending to the side effects of disease as well as their fundamental causes. In this investigation, we dive into the universe of coordinating comprehensive treatments, looking at the standards, advantages, and contemplations of this methodology.

Standards of Integrative Comprehensive Treatments

Integrative comprehensive treatments are directed by a few key standards:

1. **Comprehensive quality:** The center guideline of all encompassing treatments is comprehensive quality, which sees the person all in all, taking into account their actual wellbeing as well as their psychological, profound, and otherworldly prosperity. It perceives that these perspectives are interconnected and assume a huge part in by and large wellbeing.
2. **Personalization:** Integrative comprehensive treatments underscore individualized care. Every individual's necessities, inclinations, and conditions are considered while planning a treatment plan. Treatments are customized to address the particular wellbeing objectives and worries of the person.
3. **Avoidance:** Integrative treatments frequently center around forestalling ailment and keeping up with wellbeing. This incorporates way of life alterations, dietary decisions, and stress the executives to proactively support wellbeing and prosperity.
4. **Strengthening:** People are urged to partake in their recuperating cycle effectively. They are given apparatuses and information to arrive at informed conclusions about their wellbeing and prosperity.
5. **Joint effort:** Integrative comprehensive treatments frequently include cooperation between traditional clinical experts and all encompassing medical

services suppliers. This multidisciplinary approach guarantees that all parts of a singular's wellbeing are thought of.

Advantages of Integrative Comprehensive Treatments

The coordination of comprehensive treatments into medical services offers a few likely advantages:

1. **Complete Consideration:** Integrative all encompassing treatments address the entire individual, giving a more thorough way to deal with wellbeing and health. This can prompt a more profound comprehension of the hidden reasons for medical problems.
2. **Upgraded Prosperity:** Numerous people track down that coordinating comprehensive treatments into their medical services routine prompts expanded imperativeness, decreased pressure, and worked on profound and mental prosperity.
3. **Worked on Personal satisfaction:** Integrative treatments can upgrade the personal satisfaction for people managing constant circumstances or difficult ailments. They might assist with overseeing side effects, decrease results of medicines, and work on generally solace.
4. **Strengthening:** Integrative treatments engage people to play a functioning job in their wellbeing. They gain a feeling of command over their prosperity and are better prepared to settle on informed conclusions about their medical care.
5. **Customized Approach:** Integrative all encompassing treatments offer a customized way to deal with wellbeing, considering individual inclinations, convictions, and objectives. This can prompt seriously fulfilling and viable medical services encounters.

Contemplations for Mix

Coordinating all encompassing treatments into one's medical services routine requires cautious thought and arranging. Here are a few significant variables to remember:

1. **Correspondence:** It's critical to discuss transparently with all medical services suppliers engaged with your consideration. Ensure they know about the comprehensive treatments you are utilizing to guarantee there are no struggles or contraindications with different medicines.
2. **Proof Based Practices:** While numerous comprehensive treatments have shown guarantee in advancing prosperity, it's fundamental for look for proof based rehearses and qualified experts. Research the treatments you are thinking about and talk with legitimate experts.
3. **Security:** Guarantee that the comprehensive treatments you pick are protected

and suitable for your particular medical issue. Examine any expected dangers or worries with your medical care suppliers.
4. **Cooperation:** Support joint effort between your customary clinical experts and all encompassing medical care suppliers. This can prompt a more planned and powerful way to deal with your wellbeing.
5. **Individual Objectives:** Explain your wellbeing objectives and needs. What are you wanting to accomplish through the coordination of comprehensive treatments? Understanding your targets will direct your decisions and treatment plan.

Instances of All encompassing Treatments for Combination

Integrative comprehensive treatments include a large number of practices. Here are a few models that people frequently incorporate into their medical services schedules:

1. **Needle therapy:** Utilized for torment the board, stress decrease, and different medical issue.
2. **Care and Contemplation:** Advance unwinding, decrease pressure, and improve mental and profound prosperity.
3. **Home grown Medication:** Uses regular solutions for different wellbeing concerns.
4. **Chiropractic Care:** Spotlights on the outer muscle framework and agony the board.
5. **Sustenance and Dietary Guiding:** Locations dietary decisions and their effect on wellbeing.
6. **Energy Recuperating:** Advances equilibrium and prosperity through rehearses like Reiki or Mending Contact.
7. **Yoga and Kendo:** Further develop adaptability, balance, and mental lucidity.
8. **Knead Treatment:** Lessens muscle strain, advances unwinding, and upholds physical and close to home prosperity.
9. **Fragrance based treatment:** Utilizations natural balms for unwinding and consistent encouragement.
10. **All encompassing Psychotherapy:** Coordinates customary psychotherapy with comprehensive standards, tending to mental and profound wellbeing with regards to the entire individual.

Chapter 7

Holistic Living

All encompassing living is a way of life approach that perceives the interconnectedness of all parts of life — physical, mental, close to home, and otherworldly — and tries to make equilibrium and congruity among them. It includes settling on cognizant decisions and embracing rehearses that advance wellbeing, prosperity, and a feeling of completeness in each element of life. In this thorough investigation, we dig into the universe of comprehensive living, looking at its standards, benefits, and viable methodologies for supporting your psyche, body, and soul for ideal prosperity.

Figuring out All encompassing Living

At its center, comprehensive living is tied in with regarding life all in all, as opposed to an assortment of discrete parts. It recognizes that each part of our reality is entwined and that the prosperity of one feature influences the others. Comprehensive living incorporates the accompanying key standards:

1. **Comprehensive quality:** All encompassing living stresses the interconnectedness of all parts of life. It perceives that actual wellbeing, mental clearness, close to home equilibrium, and profound satisfaction are associated and that tending to one region can have far reaching influences on the others.
2. **Counteraction:** All encompassing residing puts major areas of strength for an on avoidance and keeping up with in general wellbeing. It urges proactive measures to forestall sickness and unevenness as opposed to exclusively responding to side effects.
3. **Mind-Body-Soul Association:** Comprehensive living recognizes the significant association between the psyche, body, and soul. It perceives that close to home and otherworldly prosperity can altogether influence actual wellbeing.
4. **Equilibrium and Amicability:** The focal objective of comprehensive living is

to encourage equilibrium and congruity in each part of life. Irregularity is seen as a main driver of physical and profound pain.
5. **Taking care of oneself:** All encompassing living advances taking care of oneself as an essential part of prosperity. This incorporates rehearses that sustain the psyche, body, and soul, like care, exercise, and profound investigation.

Advantages of All encompassing Living

Embracing all encompassing living offers various advantages for people looking to improve their prosperity and by and large personal satisfaction:

1. **Worked on Actual Wellbeing:** All encompassing living energizes solid way of life decisions, including adjusted nourishment, standard activity, and preventive medical services, which can add to better actual wellbeing and essentialness.
2. **Upgraded Close to home Strength:** Comprehensive residing rehearses like care and contemplation can assist people with overseeing pressure, diminish nervousness, and improve profound flexibility.
3. **More noteworthy Mental Clearness:** Practices that help mental prosperity, like contemplation and legitimate rest, can prompt superior concentration, mental capability, and mental lucidity.
4. **Expanded Energy:** By feeding the body with healthy food and taking part in normal active work, comprehensive living can support energy levels and battle weakness.
5. **Profound Satisfaction:** Investigating otherworldliness and interfacing with one's internal identity can give a feeling of motivation, inward harmony, and otherworldly satisfaction.
6. **Improved Connections:** All encompassing living encourages mindfulness and the capacity to understand people at their core, which can prompt better associations with oneself as well as other people.
7. **Diminished Hazard of Constant Disease:** By zeroing in on counteraction and a comprehensive way to deal with wellbeing, people might decrease their gamble of creating persistent sicknesses and experience a greater of life.

Viable Procedures for Comprehensive Living

Comprehensive living includes many practices and systems that people can integrate into their day to day routines to advance prosperity. Here are a few viable ways to deal with comprehensive living:

1. **Care and Reflection:** Develop care through everyday contemplation or careful exercises like profound breathing activities, yoga, or Jujitsu. Care can assist

with decreasing pressure, improve mental clearness, and advance profound prosperity.
2. **Adjusted Sustenance:** Focus on entire, supplement thick food varieties that sustain the body. Consolidate different natural products, vegetables, entire grains, lean proteins, and sound fats into your eating regimen.
3. **Normal Activity:** Take part in standard actual work that you appreciate, whether it's strolling, running, swimming, moving, or rehearsing yoga. Practice upholds actual wellbeing as well as lifts state of mind and mental lucidity.
4. **Satisfactory Rest:** Focus on supportive rest by keeping a reliable rest plan and establishing a rest helpful climate. Quality rest is fundamental for physical and mental prosperity.
5. **Close to home Prosperity:** Practice profound taking care of oneself by recognizing and handling your sentiments. Look for help from companions, family, or a specialist when required.
6. **Otherworldly Investigation:** Investigate your profound convictions and practices that impact you, whether through coordinated religion, contemplation, nature, or individual reflection.
7. **Careful Eating:** Practice careful eating by appreciating each nibble, eating gradually, and focusing on craving and totality signs. This can prompt better dietary patterns and a more profound association with the food you eat.
8. **Comprehensive Medical care:** Think about correlative and elective treatments, like needle therapy, natural medication, or chiropractic care, related to customary clinical therapies.
9. **Stress Decrease:** Integrate pressure decrease procedures into your day to day everyday practice, for example, journaling, profound breathing activities, or investing energy in nature.
10. **Association and Local area:** Cultivate significant associations with others and participate in exercises that give you pleasure and a feeling of having a place.
11. **Innovativeness and Articulation:** Investigate inventive outlets that permit you to put yourself out there, whether through craftsmanship, music, composing, or some other type of self-articulation.
12. **Natural Awareness:** Embrace eco-accommodating practices that advance supportability and care for the climate, like diminishing waste, monitoring energy, and supporting maintainable items.
13. **All encompassing Taking care of oneself:** Focus on taking care of oneself customs that sustain your brain, body, and soul. This might incorporate self-reflection, self-empathy, and exercises that give you pleasure and unwinding.

7.1 Creating a Holistic Home Environment

A comprehensive home climate is one that perceives and addresses the interconnectedness of physical, mental, profound, and otherworldly prosperity inside the spaces where we reside. It is a cognizant and deliberate way to deal with planning and orchestrating our homes to advance equilibrium, concordance, and by and large wellbeing in all parts of life. By imbuing your living space with comprehensive standards and practices, you can establish a sustaining climate that upholds your prosperity and improves your day to day existence. In this investigation, we dive into the craft of establishing an all encompassing home climate, looking at its standards, benefits, and commonsense procedures for changing your residing space into a safe-haven of prosperity.

Standards of a Comprehensive Home Climate

A comprehensive home climate is directed by a few key standards:

1. **Equilibrium and Congruity:** A comprehensive home tries to accomplish equilibrium and concordance among its components. It perceives that equilibrium in one everyday issue can decidedly affect different regions, prompting a feeling of by and large prosperity.
2. **Care:** Care in the home includes being available and deliberate in your decisions and activities. It implies choosing components, tones, and game plans that advance mindfulness and prosperity.
3. **Association with Nature:** All encompassing living perceives the significance of interfacing with nature. Integrating normal materials, plants, and regular light into your home climate can encourage a more profound association with the regular world.
4. **Energy Stream:** A comprehensive home is intended to permit positive energy to stream unreservedly through the space. It limits mess and obstructions to empower a feeling of stream and receptiveness.
5. **Personalization:** Imbue your home with components that mirror your qualities, interests, and otherworldliness. Personalization makes a space that reverberates with your one of a kind character and supports your general prosperity.

Advantages of an All encompassing Home Climate

Embracing an all encompassing way to deal with your home climate offers various advantages for your prosperity and personal satisfaction:

1. **Improved Mental Lucidity:** A messiness free and efficient space can add to mental clearness, permitting you to think all the more plainly and go with better choices.
2. **Profound Prosperity:** The atmosphere and style of your home can essentially influence your profound state. An agreeable and quieting climate can advance sensations of harmony, satisfaction, and solace.
3. **Actual Wellbeing:** Your home can uphold your actual wellbeing by giving a

spotless, safe, and supporting space. It can likewise energize sound propensities, for example, getting ready nutritious feasts.
4. **Stress Decrease:** A very much planned and coordinated home can act as a retreat from the burdens of day to day existence, permitting you to unwind, re-energize, and lessen pressure.
5. **Association with Otherworldliness:** By consolidating components that mirror your profound convictions and values, your home can turn into a consecrated space for reflection, contemplation, and profound development.

Useful Techniques for Establishing an All encompassing Home Climate

Changing your living space into an all encompassing safe-haven includes deliberate decisions and plan contemplations. Here are down to earth methodologies to assist you with establishing an all encompassing home climate:

1. **Clean up and Improve:** Start by cleaning up your living space. Getting out pointless things makes a feeling of receptiveness and permits energy to stream all the more unreservedly.
2. **Regular Components:** Integrate normal components into your home, like wood, stone, and plants. These components can interface you with the regular world and advance a feeling of prosperity.
3. **Variety Brain science:** Pick colors that resound with the mind-set you need to make in each room. Delicate, relieving varieties can encourage unwinding, while dynamic tones can stimulate and motivate.
4. **Careful Plans:** Organize furniture and stylistic layout carefully. Consider the progression of energy in each room and how it upholds your exercises and prosperity.
5. **Individual Touch:** Inject your home with individual contacts that mirror your inclinations, values, and otherworldliness. Show significant craftsmanship, antiquities, or images that impact you.
6. **Lighting:** Improve regular light whenever the situation allows. Regular light emphatically affects state of mind and energy. Moreover, utilize delicate, warm lighting in the nights to make a comfortable and loosening up climate.
7. **Eco-Accommodating Decisions:** Pick eco-accommodating materials and items for your home, from ground surface and furniture to cleaning supplies. Practical decisions support both your prosperity and the climate.
8. **Careful Eating Space:** Make a careful eating space in your kitchen or feasting region. Commit this space to getting a charge out of feasts without interruptions, encouraging a more profound association with your food and sustenance.
9. **Contemplation and Reflection Spaces:** Assign a peaceful corner or space for

reflection, reflection, or otherworldly practice. Occupy this space with articles and stylistic layout that move inward harmony and examination.
10. **Advanced Detox Zones:** Lay out computerized detox zones in your home where electronic gadgets are restricted or denied. These regions can give reprieve from the steady feeling of innovation.
11. **Vegetation:** Integrate houseplants into your home to further develop air quality and bring the advantages of nature inside.

7.2 Sustainable Living Practices

Maintainable living practices are a lifestyle that focuses on the wellbeing and prosperity of the two people and the planet. They include settling on cognizant decisions and taking on ways of behaving that limit damage to the climate while advancing individual and aggregate prosperity. Reasonable living recognizes the interconnectedness of human wellbeing and the soundness of the Earth, perceiving that our activities have expansive results. In this investigation, we dive into the universe of feasible living works on, looking at their standards, benefits, and down to earth procedures for sustaining the planet and ourselves.

Standards of Feasible Living

Feasible living practices are directed by a few key standards:

1. **Natural Stewardship:** Practical living perceives the significance of dealing with the Earth and its environments. It includes mindful asset the executives and endeavors to diminish natural mischief.
2. **Protection:** Preservation is at the core of supportable living. It energizes the dependable utilization of assets, like water, energy, and normal materials, to limit squander and natural effect.
3. **Equilibrium and Amicability:** Supportable living tries to accomplish equilibrium and concordance between human requirements and the necessities of the planet. It plans to guarantee that people in the future can likewise partake in a solid and flourishing climate.
4. **Independence:** Independence is a vital part of supportability. It includes diminishing reliance on impractical frameworks and making progress toward confidence in regions like food creation, energy age, and waste decrease.
5. **Local area and Coordinated effort:** Reasonable living frequently includes co-operation with similar people and networks. Cooperating to make maintainable arrangements can prompt more critical and enduring positive effects.

Advantages of Supportable Living Practices

Embracing supportable living practices offers various advantages for people, networks, and the planet:

1. **Ecological Conservation:** Feasible practices assist with lessening contamination, preserve normal assets, and safeguard environments, adding to a better planet for people in the future.
2. **Cost Reserve funds:** Numerous economical practices, like energy effectiveness and waste decrease, can prompt expense reserve funds for people and networks.
3. **Wellbeing and Prosperity:** Manageable living frequently includes better decisions, like eating privately developed, natural food and decreasing openness to hurtful synthetic compounds, prompting further developed wellbeing and prosperity.
4. **Flexibility:** Reasonable practices can increment strength despite ecological difficulties, for example, environmental change and asset shortage.
5. **Association with Nature:** Maintainable living urges a more profound association with the normal world, cultivating a feeling of marvel and appreciation for the World's excellence and variety.

Commonsense Techniques for Reasonable Living

Changing your way of life to embrace maintainability includes settling on cognizant decisions and taking on supportable practices. Here are viable procedures for economical living:

1. **Decrease, Reuse, Reuse:** Embrace the "diminish, reuse, reuse" mantra to limit squander. Lessen utilization, reuse things whenever the situation allows, and reuse materials like paper, plastic, and glass.
2. **Energy Proficiency:** Further develop energy productivity in your home by utilizing Drove lighting, fixing holes and breaks, and utilizing programmable indoor regulators. Consider environmentally friendly power sources like sunlight based chargers.
3. **Manageable Transportation:** Pick eco-accommodating transportation choices like strolling, trekking, carpooling, or utilizing public travel. Consider electric or mixture vehicles when achievable.
4. **Water Protection:** Ration water by fixing spills, introducing low-stream installations, and utilizing water-saving machines. Gather water for outside use.
5. **Maintainable Food Decisions:** Pick privately obtained, natural, and reasonably delivered food sources. Decrease meat utilization and investigate plant-based abstains from food.
6. **Eco-Accommodating Shopping:** Be aware of your buying propensities. Pick items with insignificant bundling, and backing organizations with feasible practices.
7. **Planting and Horticulture:** Develop your food in a nursery or on a little

homestead, if conceivable. Utilize reasonable cultivating practices like natural cultivating, crop turn, and fertilizing the soil.
8. **Diminish Single-Use Things:** Limit the utilization of single-use plastics and expendable items. Utilize reusable packs, compartments, and utensils.
9. **Cognizant Commercialization:** Pursue smart decisions about what you purchase and consume. Think about the ecological effect of your buys and their life span.
10. **Local area Inclusion:** Draw in with neighborhood local area associations and drives zeroed in on maintainability. Join or care groups that advance economical living practices.
11. **Instruction and Mindfulness:** Remain informed about ecological issues and maintainability through books, narratives, and news sources. Share information and motivate others to embrace reasonable practices.
12. **Moderation:** Embrace a moderate way of life by cleaning up and improving on your assets. Center around better standards without compromise and diminish superfluous utilization.

7.3 Nurturing Relationships and Social Wellness

Social health is an indispensable part of generally prosperity that underscores the nature of our connections, social associations, and collaborations with others. Supporting connections and cultivating social wellbeing assume a pivotal part in our psychological, close to home, and actual wellbeing. These associations add to a feeling of having a place, backing, and reason, eventually upgrading our general personal satisfaction. In this investigation, we dig into the significance of supporting connections and developing social health, analyzing their standards, benefits, and pragmatic procedures for building significant associations.

Standards of Sustaining Connections and Social Wellbeing

Supporting connections and social wellbeing are directed by a few key standards:

1. **Association:** Social health is attached in the capacity to interface with others on a significant level. It includes fabricating and keeping an organization of connections that offer help, friendship, and a feeling of having a place.
2. **Correspondence:** Successful correspondence is fundamental for sustaining connections. It incorporates undivided attention, offering viewpoints and sentiments genuinely, and rehearsing sympathy to grasp others' points of view.
3. **Common Regard:** Regard is the underpinning of solid connections. It includes esteeming each other's disparities, limits, and independence.
4. **Trust:** Trust is a principal component of any solid relationship. It is created through consistency, dependability, and open correspondence.
5. **Everyday encouragement:** Giving and getting consistent reassurance is a basic

part of social wellbeing. It includes being there for others during testing times and looking for help when required.

Advantages of Sustaining Connections and Social Health

Embracing the standards of sustaining connections and social wellbeing offers various advantages for people and networks:

1. **Close to home:** Areas of strength for prosperity associations are related with worked on profound prosperity, including lower levels of pressure, uneasiness, and melancholy.
2. **Expanded Bliss:** Significant connections add to a more prominent feeling of joy and life fulfillment.
3. Worked on Actual Wellbeing: Social wellbeing is connected to better actual wellbeing results, including lower pulse and a diminished gamble of constant illnesses.
4. **Upgraded Strength:** Strong connections give a cradle against life's difficulties, improving versatility and abilities to adapt.
5. **Feeling of Having a place:** Feeling associated with others cultivates a feeling of having a place and reason, diminishing sensations of disconnection.

Functional Systems for Supporting Connections and Social Wellbeing

Constructing and keeping up with sound connections require goal, exertion, and powerful correspondence. Here are commonsense techniques for sustaining connections and upgrading social health:

1. **Focus on Higher standards no matter what:** Spotlight on developing a couple of significant connections as opposed to extending yourself excessively far. Quality associations frequently give more critical advantages.
2. **Undivided attention:** Practice undivided attention by focusing completely on the speaker, posing explaining inquiries, and approving their sentiments.
3. **Impart Straightforwardly:** Cultivate transparent correspondence in your connections. Share your contemplations, sentiments, and worries while additionally reassuring others to do likewise.
4. **Offer Thanks:** Offer appreciation and thanks to the people who assume a positive part in your life. Little tokens of appreciation can fortify connections.
5. **Put down Stopping points:** Lay out solid limits in your connections to safeguard your prosperity and regard the limits of others.
6. **Look for Shared Interests:** Take part in exercises and leisure activities that line up with your inclinations and values, improving the probability of meeting similar people.

7. **Network and Mingle:** Go to get-togethers, join clubs or associations, and take part in local area exercises to grow your interpersonal organization.
8. **Volunteer:** Chipping in furnishes a valuable chance to interface with other people who share your enthusiasm for a specific reason while having a beneficial outcome on your local area.
9. **Reconnect:** Reconnect with lifelong companions and colleagues to renew past connections and make new recollections.
10. **Be Strong:** Offer everyday reassurance to companions and friends and family during testing times, and make sure to help when you want it.
11. **Compassion:** Practice sympathy by imagining others' perspective and attempting to figure out their sentiments and points of view.
12. **Retouch Connections:** Address clashes and errors in a useful way to repair and fortify harmed connections.

Chapter 8

The Holistic Journey Ahead

The Comprehensive Excursion Ahead: Exploring Life's Way to Prosperity

Life is an excursion, a perplexing and interconnected embroidery of encounters, feelings, and difficulties. At its center, this excursion is an investigation of prosperity, including the physical, mental, close to home, and profound components of our reality. The comprehensive excursion ahead welcomes us to explore this perplexing way deliberately, sustaining our psyche, body, and soul to accomplish a condition of significant prosperity. In this far reaching investigation, we dive into the comprehensive excursion, analyzing its standards, pragmatic systems, and the significant changes it can bring to our lives.

Grasping the Comprehensive Excursion

The comprehensive excursion is established on the acknowledgment that our prosperity is an unpredictable web, with each aspect of our reality interconnected. It recognizes that actual wellbeing, mental clearness, profound equilibrium, and otherworldly satisfaction are reliant and that tending to one region can have expanding influences on the others. The comprehensive excursion is directed by a few center standards:

1. **Comprehensive quality**

    At the core of the comprehensive excursion is comprehensive quality, the conviction that all that in our lives is interconnected. It highlights that our prosperity can't be compartmentalized; all things considered, it's the cooperative energy of our physical, mental, close to home, and otherworldly selves that adds to our general condition of wellbeing and joy.

2. **Anticipation**

    The comprehensive excursion underscores counteraction as a useful asset for keeping up with prosperity. As opposed to just responding to side effects and diseases, it urges proactive measures to forestall sickness and awkwardness in any case. Counteraction includes settling on careful decisions about nourishment, work out, stress the board, and that's just the beginning.

3. **Equilibrium and Concordance**
Accomplishing equilibrium and concordance in all parts of life is a focal objective of the comprehensive excursion. Irregularity is viewed as a main driver of physical and profound trouble, and the excursion looks to reestablish harmony by tending to both inner and outer variables.

4. **Mind-Body-Soul Association**
The all encompassing excursion perceives the significant association between the brain, body, and soul. It comprehends that close to home and profound prosperity can essentially influence actual wellbeing as well as the other way around. Developing this association is fundamental for all encompassing prosperity.

5. **Taking care of oneself**

Taking care of oneself is key in the comprehensive excursion. It includes rehearses that sustain the brain, body, and soul. Taking care of oneself envelops exercises like care, work out, otherworldly investigation, and close to home taking care of oneself.

Advantages of Embracing the Comprehensive Excursion

Embracing the all encompassing excursion offers a huge number of advantages for people looking to improve their prosperity and personal satisfaction. Here are a portion of the striking benefits:

1. **Worked on Actual Wellbeing**
Comprehensive living energizes sound way of life decisions, including adjusted sustenance, ordinary activity, and preventive medical care. This adds to better actual wellbeing, imperativeness, and versatility against sickness.

2. **Improved Close to home Flexibility**
Rehearses like care and reflection, key to the all encompassing excursion, engage people to oversee pressure, decrease tension, and improve profound flexibility. This profound strength supports exploring life's difficulties with beauty and composure.

3. **More noteworthy Mental Lucidity**
Rehearses that help mental prosperity, like reflection and legitimate rest, lead to further developed center, mental capability, and mental clearness. An unmistakable brain is better prepared to pursue informed choices and explore life's intricacies.

4. **Expanded Energy**
Sustaining the body with healthy food and taking part in normal actual work, as pushed in the comprehensive excursion, supports energy levels and

battles exhaustion. This uplifted energy works with efficiency and a feeling of essentialness.
5. **Profound Satisfaction**
Investigating otherworldliness and interfacing with one's internal identity can give a profound feeling of motivation, inward harmony, and otherworldly satisfaction. This part of the all encompassing excursion can significantly improve one's life.
6. **Upgraded Connections**
Comprehensive living cultivates mindfulness and the capacity to appreciate anyone on a profound level, characteristics that add to better associations with oneself as well as other people. Further developed correspondence and compassion upgrade the nature of associations.
7. **Diminished Hazard of Constant Disease**

By zeroing in on counteraction and embracing a comprehensive way to deal with wellbeing, people might lessen their gamble of creating constant sicknesses. This broadens future as well as upgrades the personal satisfaction.

Exploring the Comprehensive Excursion: Useful Procedures

The comprehensive excursion is definitely not a theoretical idea however a way that can be crossed with intentional advances and activities. Here are viable techniques to explore this excursion:

1. **Care and Reflection**
Develop care through day to day contemplation or careful exercises like profound breathing activities, yoga, or Kendo. Care upgrades mindfulness, decreases pressure, and advances profound prosperity.
2. **Adjusted Nourishment**
Focus on entire, supplement thick food sources that support the body. Integrate different organic products, vegetables, entire grains, lean proteins, and sound fats into your eating regimen.
3. **Standard Activity**
Participate in normal actual work that you appreciate, whether it's strolling, running, swimming, moving, or rehearsing yoga. Practice upholds actual wellbeing as well as lifts mind-set and mental clearness.
4. **Satisfactory Rest**
Focus on supportive rest by keeping a predictable rest plan and establishing a rest helpful climate. Quality rest is fundamental for physical and mental prosperity.
5. **Profound Prosperity**
Practice close to home taking care of oneself by recognizing and handling

your sentiments. Look for help from companions, family, or a specialist when required.

6. **Profound Investigation**
   Investigate your profound convictions and practices that impact you, whether through coordinated religion, contemplation, nature, or individual reflection.

7. **Careful Eating**
   Practice careful eating by enjoying each chomp, eating gradually, and focusing on craving and completion signals. This can prompt better dietary patterns and a more profound association with the food you devour.

8. **Comprehensive Medical care**
   Think about correlative and elective treatments, like needle therapy, natural medication, or chiropractic care, related to customary clinical medicines.

9. **Stress Decrease**
   Integrate pressure decrease methods into your everyday daily schedule, for example, journaling, profound breathing activities, or investing energy in nature.

10. **Association and Local area**
    Encourage significant associations with others and participate in exercises that give you pleasure and a feeling of having a place.

11. **Imagination and Articulation**
    Investigate imaginative outlets that permit you to articulate your thoughts, whether through craftsmanship, music, composing, or some other type of self-articulation.

12. **Ecological Cognizance**
    Take on eco-accommodating practices that advance supportability and care for the climate, like decreasing waste, monitoring energy, and supporting manageable items.

13. **All encompassing Taking care of oneself**

Focus on taking care of oneself customs that support your psyche, body, and soul. This might incorporate self-reflection, self-sympathy, and exercises that give you pleasure and unwinding.

The All encompassing Excursion: A Long lasting Investigation

The comprehensive excursion isn't an objective yet a long lasting investigation and obligation to supporting your psyche, body, and soul for ideal prosperity. An excursion develops as you develop, learn, and adjust to life's steadily evolving scene. Whether you look for actual imperativeness, profound flexibility, mental lucidity, or otherworldly development, the comprehensive excursion offers an all encompassing way to sustaining each element of your being.

In the pages that follow, we leave on a top to bottom investigation of the all encompassing excursion ahead. We will dive into each element of prosperity —

physical, mental, profound, and otherworldly — and reveal reasonable systems, experiences, and insight to direct you on your way to all encompassing prosperity. Together, we will explore the multifaceted embroidery of life's excursion, cultivating a condition of significant prosperity and satisfaction.

8.1 Overcoming Challenges

Defeating Difficulties: The Way to Versatility and Development

Life is a mind boggling venture loaded up with both delights and preliminaries. Challenges are an unavoidable piece of this excursion, and they come in different structures, from individual mishaps to outside snags. How we answer and defeat these difficulties can significantly shape our personality, strength, and self-awareness. In this investigation, we dive into the craft of conquering difficulties, looking at the standards, benefits, and functional procedures for exploring difficulty with elegance and assurance.

Standards of Conquering Difficulties

Conquering difficulties is directed by a few key standards:

1. **Versatility:** Strength is the capacity to return quickly from difficulty. It includes creating profound and mental solidarity to successfully adapt to hardships and misfortunes.
2. **Flexibility:** Difficulties frequently expect us to adjust and really impact our systems or mentality. Being available to transformation is urgent for beating impediments.
3. **Positive Mentality:** A positive outlook enables us to consider difficulties to be open doors for development. It includes reexamining misfortunes as growth opportunities and keeping up with good faith notwithstanding affliction.
4. **Critical thinking:** Compelling critical thinking abilities are fundamental for conquering difficulties. It includes separating complex issues into reasonable advances and looking for arrangements earnestly.
5. **Self-Sympathy:** Self-empathy is the act of treating oneself with benevolence and understanding during troublesome times. It includes recognizing our own battles and offering ourselves similar sympathy we would to a companion.

Advantages of Conquering Difficulties

Embracing difficulties and managing them offers various advantages:

1. **Self-awareness:** Conquering difficulties frequently prompts self-awareness, expanded mindfulness, and a more noteworthy feeling of versatility.
2. **Certainty:** Effectively exploring difficulties fabricates self-assurance and a faith in one's capacity to confront future deterrents.
3. **Versatility:** The capacity to adjust and issue settle even with difficulties upgrades flexibility and genius.

4. **Sympathy:** Beating individual difficulties can prompt more prominent compassion and comprehension of others' battles.
5. **Accomplishment:** Each challenge vanquished brings a pride and fulfillment, spurring us to handle new objectives.

Viable Methodologies for Conquering Difficulties

Exploring difficulties requires intentional and compelling methodologies. Here are down to earth moves toward assist you with beating affliction:

1. **Characterize the Test:** Obviously characterize the test you're confronting. Separate it into more modest, sensible parts to make it less overpowering.
2. **Look for Help:** Contact companions, family, or care groups for daily encouragement and point of view. Sharing your test can ease up the close to home weight.
3. **Foster an Arrangement:** Make an organized arrangement to address the test. Put forth clear objectives and distinguish stages to accomplish them.
4. **Remain Positive:** Develop a positive mentality by zeroing in on arrangements as opposed to harping on issues. Practice appreciation and keep a hopeful viewpoint.
5. **Taking care of oneself:** Focus on taking care of oneself to fabricate physical and profound flexibility. Get sufficient rest, eat sustaining food varieties, work out, and take part in unwinding strategies.
6. **Learn and Adjust:** Move toward difficulties as learning open doors. Be available to adjusting your methodologies and looking for new abilities or information.
7. **Fabricate Versatility:** Reinforce your strength by rehearsing care, reflection, and other pressure decrease methods. These practices assist you with returning quickly from misfortunes all the more successfully.
8. **Endure:** Determination is critical to defeating difficulties. Continue to push ahead, in any event, when progress appears to be slow or mishaps happen.
9. **Remain Adaptable:** Be adaptable and open to change. In some cases, the way to defeating a test might require changing your methodology.
10. **Observe Little Wins:** Recognize and praise your advancement, regardless of how little. Perceiving your accomplishments helps inspiration and confidence.
11. **Look for Proficient Assistance:** In the event that the test is especially complicated or overpowering, think about looking for direction from an advisor, guide, or mentor who has practical experience in the space of your test.
12. **Keep up with Viewpoint:** Recall that difficulties are a piece of life, and they don't characterize your value or capacities. Remember the master plan.

8.2 Sustaining Holistic Wellness

Supporting Comprehensive Health: Sustaining a Long period of Prosperity

Comprehensive health isn't an objective yet a long lasting excursion. It incorporates the interconnected components of physical, mental, close to home, and profound prosperity, and it is a promise to supporting these viewpoints all through one's life. Supporting all encompassing wellbeing requires a persistent and purposeful work to focus on taking care of oneself, settle on careful decisions, and adjust to life's steadily evolving conditions. In this investigation, we dive into the craft of supporting comprehensive health, looking at the standards, benefits, and reasonable techniques for feeding prosperity all through a lifetime.

Standards of Supporting All encompassing Wellbeing

Supporting all encompassing wellbeing is directed by a few center standards:

1. **Ceaseless Development:** All encompassing wellbeing is an excursion of nonstop development and personal growth. It recognizes that self-improvement and prosperity are continuous cycles.
2. **Equilibrium and Concordance:** Supporting prosperity includes keeping up with equilibrium and agreement among the different elements of health. It perceives that ignoring one perspective can influence the general personal satisfaction.
3. **Taking care of oneself as Vital:** Focusing on taking care of oneself is principal to supporting all encompassing wellbeing. Taking care of oneself practices are not extravagances but rather fundamental parts of keeping up with prosperity.
4. **Versatility:** Life is dynamic, and supporting health requires flexibility. It includes acclimating to evolving conditions, laying out new objectives, and reexamining taking care of oneself schedules depending on the situation.
5. **Careful Decisions:** Supporting comprehensive wellbeing includes settling on careful decisions in all parts of life, from sustenance and active work to connections and stress the board.

Advantages of Supporting All encompassing Wellbeing

Embracing and supporting all encompassing wellbeing over the course of life offers various advantages:

1. **Life span:** Focusing on prosperity can prompt a more extended and better life, decreasing the gamble of persistent sicknesses and upgrading generally essentialness.
2. **Upgraded Personal satisfaction:** Supporting comprehensive wellbeing adds to a superior personal satisfaction by cultivating actual wellbeing, mental lucidity, profound strength, and otherworldly satisfaction.
3. **Strength:** Nonstop taking care of oneself and prosperity rehearses improve

flexibility, empowering people to all the more likely explore life's difficulties and recuperate from misfortunes.
4. **Internal Harmony:** All encompassing health cultivates inward harmony and a feeling of direction, adding to a really satisfying and satisfied life.
5. **Positive Connections:** Supporting prosperity can prompt better and more sure associations with oneself as well as other people.
6. **Individual Satisfaction:** Supporting comprehensive wellbeing advances individual satisfaction by adjusting one's life to their qualities and desires.

Pragmatic Techniques for Supporting All encompassing Health

Supporting comprehensive wellbeing includes focusing on health and incorporating it into day to day existence. Here are pragmatic techniques to assist you with supporting all encompassing prosperity:

1. **Reliable Taking care of oneself:** Focus on steady taking care of oneself works on, including standard activity, care, and satisfactory rest.
2. **Adjusted Sustenance:** Keep a fair and feeding diet by consolidating different entire food sources. Remain hydrated and limit handled and undesirable decisions.
3. **Work-out Consistently:** Participate in customary active work that you appreciate. Practice advances actual wellbeing as well as upgrades mental and profound prosperity.
4. **Profound Mindfulness:** Develop close to home mindfulness and flexibility by recognizing and handling your sentiments. Look for help when required.
5. **Profound Investigation:** Keep investigating your otherworldliness and associating with your internal identity through contemplation, supplication, or different practices that impact you.
6. **Long lasting Learning:** Cultivate an outlook of deep rooted learning and self-awareness. Seek after interests, gain new abilities, and remain intellectually locked in.
7. **Standard Wellbeing Tests:** Timetable normal exams with medical care experts to screen your actual wellbeing and address any issues quickly.
8. **Stress The executives:** Practice pressure the board strategies, like profound breathing, reflection, or yoga, to keep up with close to home equilibrium.
9. **Association and Local area:** Remain associated with friends and family and take part in significant social cooperations. Local area inclusion can add to a feeling of direction.
10. **Adjust to Change:** Embrace change as a characteristic piece of life and adjust your wellbeing schedules to oblige developing conditions.
11. **Put forth Objectives:** Constantly set and work toward prosperity objectives,

whether they connect with actual wellness, self-improvement, or close to home strength.
12. **Observe Achievements:** Recognize and commend achievements and accomplishments in your health process. Perceiving progress helps inspiration and supports positive propensities.
13. **Look for Help:** Make it a point to help from medical care experts, specialists, or health mentors while confronting difficulties or requiring direction.

8.3 Holistic Wellness as a Lifelong Path

All encompassing Health as a Deep rooted Way: Supporting Prosperity Across the Ages

All encompassing health is definitely not a fleeting pattern or an impermanent fix; it is a long lasting way, a significant obligation to supporting prosperity across the sum of one's presence. This excursion rises above age, including the physical, mental, close to home, and otherworldly components of prosperity from youth to the brilliant years.

Standards of All encompassing Health as a Deep rooted Way

All encompassing health as a deep rooted way is directed by a few basic standards. It, right off the bat, recognizes that prosperity is a ceaseless course of development and improvement. People, everything being equal, can obtain new information, abilities, and encounters that add to their general wellbeing. Besides, embracing change and adjusting to new conditions is an essential part of long lasting health. As life unfurls, people should change their wellbeing schedules and needs to address advancing issues.

Thirdly, all encompassing wellbeing perceives that every life stage brings its remarkable difficulties and open doors. It accentuates balance in sustaining physical, mental, close to home, and otherworldly prosperity at each age. Finally, the way of deep rooted wellbeing stresses preventive measures and proactivity. As opposed to trusting that medical problems will emerge, people find proactive ways to keep up with and improve their prosperity.

Advantages of All encompassing Health Across the Ages

Embracing all encompassing health over the course of life offers a huge number of advantages. In youth, all encompassing wellbeing encourages energy, versatility, and sound development, setting the establishment for a lively and dynamic life. During midlife, it upholds versatility and flexibility, assisting people with exploring profession changes, family obligations, and self-improvement.

In the brilliant years, comprehensive health adds to improving with age, keeping up with physical and mental dexterity, profound prosperity, and a feeling of satisfaction. At each age, it upgrades the personal satisfaction, cultivating a feeling of direction, internal harmony, and generally speaking happiness. Also, long lasting wellbeing advances progressing learning, interest, and self-improvement, enhancing's comprehension one might interpret self and the world.

Useful Methodologies for Comprehensive Wellbeing Across the Ages

Sustaining comprehensive health over the course of life includes applying commonsense techniques custom fitted to every life stage. In youth and immaturity, it's essential to energize actual work and play to advance sound development, cultivate the capacity to understand people on a profound level and flexibility through open correspondence and daily encouragement, and acquaint care and unwinding procedures with oversee pressure and construct mental clearness. In youthful adulthood, focusing on adjusted nourishment and standard activity for supported energy

is critical, alongside investigating side interests, interests, and instructive pursuits to encourage self-awareness. Developing significant connections and a solid social encouraging group of people is likewise fundamental.

In midlife, overseeing pressure actually through unwinding, care, or reflection is basic. Chasing after profession advancement and individual objectives lined up with values and goals is similarly significant, as is focusing on taking care of oneself and actual wellness to keep up with essentialness and forestall age-related medical problems.

In the brilliant years, participating in deep rooted learning and mental activities to keep the psyche sharp ought to be a concentration, alongside focusing on profound prosperity by keeping up with associations with friends and family and looking for help when required. Embracing actual work, even in changed structures, is imperative to keep up with portability and generally wellbeing.

At long last, over the course of life, it's essential to ceaselessly rethink and change wellbeing schedules to oblige changing necessities and conditions. Looking for ordinary exams and preventive medical services measures while sticking to clinical counsel is fundamental. Embracing the insight that accompanies age, considering life's excursion, and finding satisfaction right now are significant parts of supporting all encompassing wellbeing.

Printed in the USA
CPSIA information can be obtained
at www.ICGtesting.com
LVHW021205201023
761658LV00050B/624